CORPORATE SKILLS

Vikram's insight into Vet la's Management

Prof. Shrikant Prasoon

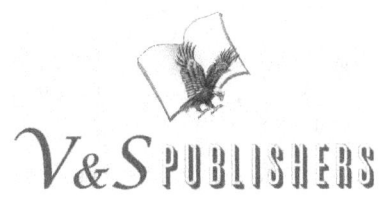

V&S PUBLISHERS

Published by:

V&S PUBLISHERS

F-2/16, Ansari Road, Daryaganj, New Delhi-110002
011-23240026, 011-23240027 • *Fax:* 011-23240028
Email: info@vspublishers.com • *Website:* www.vspublishers.com

Branch : Hyderabad
5-1-707/1, Brij Bhawan (Beside Central Bank of India Lane)
Bank Street, Koti, Hyderabad - 500 095
040-24737290
E-mail: vspublishershyd@gmail.com

Follow us on:

For any assistance sms **VSPUB** to **56161**

All books available at **www.vspublishers.com**

© **Copyright:** *V&S PUBLISHERS*
ISBN 978-93-815889-6-3
Edition 2013

Printed at : Param Offseters, Okhla, New Delhi-110020

Contents

Preface

CORPORATE SKILLS – Vikram's insight into Vetāla's Management' is based on the famous stories of Vikram and Vetāla with practical tips on Management. It contains all the stories as they have been originally told. They are the translations of the Sanskrit Text. There is no mutilation to suit the end in mind. The ingredients of modern management are very much present in it.

At a number of places it mentions about the ancient period during that ancient period itself. In a way, it is a claim that it was modern in its own time and in its own way. Its modernity is still alive and effective. Hence, its ancient modernity will help the modern executives to unite themselves to the ever growing and lively roots of Indian Management Techniques.

Because of the questions at the end of every story, some people claim it to be Riddles. By telling Riddles they try to create mystery around it. But the questions are straightway related to morality, ethics, character, courage, charity, kindness, compassion, pity, religiosity, and other great human values.

If they are kept as plain questions our own morality and ethics, the inner being and the real character comes to fore; and can be questioned. It is up to the humans to prove that they are human.

That is the intention of the author in writing these stories. It is we who are tested; and the touchstone is the answer and logic given by the great and just ruler Vikram or Mahārājā Vikramāditya, on whose lost throne, when found, and when another great and just king Rājā Bhoja wished to go up and sit; the Putalies (Figurines), created at each step, stopped him, tested him every day by telling valorous deeds of Mahārājā Vikramāditya and on the 32nd day he was able to sit on the throne.

If a just king can be tested and asked to prove his human and sublime character then others cannot be spared. The stories and the answers hit our conscience hard. So, these are great, meaningful and important stories;

very apt for modern man. The greatness and the meaning and the essence of these stories lie in Morality, Ethics, Humanity and Religiosity.

Different aspects and riddles of the 25 stories of Vikram and Vetāla have been analysed and explained in the context of modern management. Hence, it will work as a Troubleshooter, a very common post in the field of management in the USA.

'CORPORATE SKILLS – Vikram's insight into Vetāla's Management' will be of immense help in managing successfully an organization of any magnitude: macro organization or micro organization; personal or public organization. It will give an insight into its different problems; show their magnitude and dimension and present reliable and practical solutions: both broad and subtle; as it is a practical approach to the nuisances of management.

An executive looks for notions, intelligence and purpose
He cannot work on wasteful emotions or intentions dubious
In place of bowing down to passion he prefers rational ways
Stimulates creativity, growth, gain and accumulates surplus.

All the **Quadruplets**, the poems of only four lines quoted at the beginning of each chapter; in which 1st, 2nd, and 4th lines rhyme together (as one quoted above); and the lines are repeated while reciting (not reading, as poetry should always be recited.); have been taken from the writer's anthology "**Spiritual Quadruplets.**"

All the **Quotes** given at the end of every chapter have been taken from the writer's collection of quotations.

Only ā from Scriptural Transliteration have been used to denote long 'a' sound, so that the readers can easily read and understand different names of persons and places and other words from Hindi and Sanskrit.

– Prof. Shrikant Prasoon

Introduction

What and Why of Vikram, Vetāla and the Stories

The Purpose

The purpose behind the tales of Vikram and Vetāla is to enrich and sharpen the insight into life which will provide a balanced view; and to determine the duties of individuals towards organizations; and finally to manage **Self; Time; Family; Society** and **Empire** of one's own, howsoever, small or big.

Teachings

The Indians have added 'teachings' as an integral and essential part of writing as a whole and story-telling in particular. They teach numerous things through stories. Along with that with a very fine thread they have woven the problems of life in the stories. This is evident in these classical stories.

That is the reason why the stories Vetāla tells to Vikram are co-related to Management. *Neither the word management nor an equivalent word has been used but because these are the tales of kings and merchants so, management has to be its inseparable part.*

Lack of Insight

Indians are never superfluous with their explanation. They were great visionaries. They had insight. Modernity lacks both vision and insight. It is evident with the word Talent (Pratibhā). For them a child that sings well has talent; a man who writes an article has talent; a student who appears at a science-show has talent; and a girl who works on computer has talent and so on.

But in Indian context Pratibhā (Talent) has far deeper connotation and denotation than what the modern man thinks of it. They cannot even visualize what the Indians thought of Pratibha. Let us see:

Smritih vyatita vishayā matih āgāmigocharā;

Buddhih tatkāliki proktā pragya traikāliki matā;

Prgyam navavonmeshashālinim pratibhām biduh.

Smriti (memory) is a matter of past; *mati* (intellect) deals with future; *buddhi* (wisdom) with the present and *prgayā* (deep learning) with *Trikāla* (all the three phases of time). When the person that knows the past, present and future, starts creating new things, it's called *pratibhā* (talent).

स्मृति: व्यतीत विशया मति: आगामिगोचरा।

बुद्धि: तत्कालिकी प्रोक्ता प्रज्ञा त्रैकालिकी मता।

प्रज्ञां नवनवोन्मेषशालिनी प्रतिभां विदु:।

स्मृति का विषय अतीत है, मति का भविष्य, बुद्धि का वर्तमान और प्रज्ञा का त्रिकाल; प्रज्ञा ही जब नवनवोन्मेषशालिनी, नई-नई सर्जनाएँ करने में समर्थ होती है, तब उसे प्रतिभा कहते हैं।

(Both creative and analytical mind is needed in business and management. Accumulation and synthesis is as essential in this field as distribution and disbursement. In this regard, for better control, the knowledge of the past sales and performance, present production and distribution, and the future demands and needs must be known: even approximately if not exactly. That says volumes about wise and equipped investors, manufacturers and dealers.)

On the basis of the definitions given above hardly a few persons among millions or trillions can be called as talented. Naturally the *Shlokas* composed or the stories told or the characters created are meaningful because they had insight into the phases of time and while creating something they kept past, present and future in mind. On the contrary, most of the writings today become meaningless and useless after a few hours or days or weeks or months and definitely after a few years.

It has not happened, and it will not happen to Indian writing and not even to the twenty-five tales narrated in **Vetālapanchvinshati**.

People are after Money

Modern vision and insight is skin-deep, the outer visible reality, and their vision is limited to price rise and percentage of gain. They think in the terms of growth-percentages. Money and physical pleasure are at the center of the thought and action of modern man. It was only half of life for the Indians. Those who hankered after it lived an incomplete life. These are the two parts of the four **Human Pursuits: Dharma (Religiosity); Artha (Finance); Kāma (Sex) and Moksha (Salvation).** They miss the other two: Dharma and Moksha. What is the use of living an incomplete and dissatisfied life? It's the 'Wholeness' that counts at the end.

In this book **'Vikram's Insight into Vetāla Management'**, there is special emphasis on Artha (Finance) as a part of Management but in its totality, Management deals with the management of each diverse thing in different situations. So, it will give a sense of completeness.

People are not planning for Life

In the race for making money, people are not getting time and leisure to think of life. Man is working in shifts to make extra money and thinking in piecemeal to get rid of the health hazards and loneliness. One must think and plan how one should lead his life. On the contrary, the thinking that when there is enough money, the life will change and will be happy and peaceful is obnoxious. This is the greatest illusion. When money accumulates life takes unnatural twists and gets spoilt. Life is not led that way and from thereon. Earning and spending; getting strong and working hard, working for livelihood and supporting family; all have to work simultaneously and harmoniously. Of course, majority of the people do it successfully (more than 70 percent people still follow that path) and exercise better control over self, income and expenditure.

But the rest are all the time planning for earning more and more money and are never planning for life: forgetting to lead a healthy, happy, peaceful and prosperous life by burdening the shoulders with worries on work, skill and ability.

Warding off Monotony

Something must be done to overcome monotony and ward off tiredness caused by the routine work at the same place, in the same manner and among the same men, day in and day out and for decades. It is driving people mad. Eccentrics and criminals are born out of the mechanical milieu and work. There is no change or variation possible; if there is any, it is superfluous and temporary. Physical fatigue is a different matter. It is the mental fatigue that is playing havoc in all industrialized societies.

On the contrary, in the yester years, everything gets restarted after every season; growing better crop; different varieties of crops or for different purpose the interest remains lively. Physical tiredness may be there but there was no monotony; rather a lot of freedom was available. The routine, crop and other things can be re-adjusted. So the scope and latitude increases. That made the Indians to announce "uttam kheti"; cultivation of crops as the best employment and work.

The Creation of Vetāla and his Inner Strength

One day Devādhideva Mahādeva, Lord Shiva, was in meditation. Brahmā on Swan, and Vishnu on eagle reached there. Brahmā said, "O Lord Shiva! You have a habit of either going on penance or sitting in meditation. You should do something different."

Mahesh was pleased. He said, "Yes, I will do something different but what?"

Brahmā said again, "You should start creating new beings."

Mahesh was in ecstasy, "Yes, yes, with all pleasure."

When Brahmā and Vishnu returned Mahādeva went in deep trance and started creating new beings.

Chandrashekhar started creating new beings and created them very fast. Of course, he created the beings of his personal liking and choice. In fact, he created:

Preta: Phantoms

Pishācha: Ghosts

Bhairava: Dogs

Vināyaka: Eagles

Yatudhana: Demons

Dākini: Sorceress

Shākini: Female Demons

Kushumāndā: Pumpkins

Yogini: Female Ascetic Attendants

Vetāla: Minstrels

The moment Brahmā and Vishnu learnt about the strange creations of Jatādhāri, they rushed to him and immediately stopped him from creating more vile and dangerous creatures.

Now, it was a problem to control those unique beings. Gangādhāri was asked to control them. They were all made his Gans, called Rudra and deputed in his service. With immediate effect they were pressed into the service of their creator Lord. The Lord accepted them in his employment and fostered them with care as Rudra.

Yet, it was not easy to keep an eye on and control the strange, vile and dangerous creatures. So, Shri Ganesh was made the Ganpati, the master of all the Gans. They came under his direct control and rule. This helped the Gans. With the blessings of both Gajānan and Kailāshpati they became strong and wise without much effort.

Creation of Vetāla

The above narration shows at least three things: Vetālas are the creation of Lord Umāpati; they are ruled and controlled by Lambodar; and they possess some supernatural powers, and a part of the strength, moral character and wisdom of the one that conceived and created them and the immediate Boss. Gans are endowed with some special powers. Because of the visible and invisible physical form and supernatural ability to change their form they are able to perform strange deeds.

It is up to the immediate Boss and the Managing Director to see what the employees can do and how can they achieve the expected and desired goals within the time limit. All organizations have strange characters full of power and whims, ability and alertness, and idiosyncratic ideas and personal problems. It is up to the Management to utilise the latent talent and power in the most creative and positive way to the best advantage of the organisation for its prosperity.

Vetāla's Strength

Understanding and presenting the problems in profane way is the real strength of Vetāla. It was possible because he had the power to see both the recent past and closer future. Distant past and distant future were not under his vision and understanding. That is why Vetāla was able to raise riddle-like questions rich in insight in accordance with the incident, situation and characters.

Vetāla belongs to the rare community of spirits known as Vidyādhar. He has immense power to do unbelievable things. Shakespeare changed him into Acrial in *The Tempest* but did not forget to mention Indian sea-cost. These Vidyādhars were changed into Genie in Persian literature. Either through Persian or Vasco de Gama these Indian classics transmitted to other countries and got translated and adapted in other languages.

Vikram or Mahārājā Vikramāditya

Vikramāditya was a very sensitive, refined, polished, sublime and wise king known for his valiant deeds, great moral character and practical wisdom. His analytical power and the ability to synthesize made him formidable. He was an emblem of patience and endurance. In nutshell, he was an ideal and sublime king.

To ensure a successful and wholesome life it is imperative to understand the sublime qualities of King Vikramāditya; absorb them; follow his methods with the wisdom of that grand order. Certainly it was not re-living a myth but creating a myth altogether.

Vikram Samvat

Vikram possessed great qualities and characteristics of a highly successful man. His success can be measured from the fact that the Brahmins of his time accepted him as the most pious and wise person. So much so, they agreed on starting "Vikram Samvat" to start the fresh counting of years on the basis of the date of birth of Mahārājā Vikramāditya. It is exactly 57 years before the birth of Christ. So, Modern Indian Samvat is always 57 years ahead of Christian counting of years. If we count back from 2008, Emperor Vikramāditya was born exactly 2065 years ago, which is the present Vikram Samvat.

Given the rigidity of the Brahmins, it is a great achievement of the King that his name was accepted as the starting point of a fresh counting of years. One thing is clear, had he not been a super power, super creature and very great among the great; very wise among the wise and very pious among the pious, the resolute Brahmins would not have agreed to his name. It easily establishes the fact that Vikram has (had) no peer anywhere.

These tales written so well; show how king Vikram became Vikramāsity. After getting the bliss that the Buddha Monk was expecting to from the worshipping, sacrifices and penance, and being blessed by Lord Shiva King Vikramāditya won over the whole world and ruled over it for a long time. It was Lord Shiva that made him **Vikramāditya.**

After his departure many kings took the title of Vikramāditya. So, there are many kings with that title but only one king with that name. Some writers got confused but there should not be any confusion as he was the king who was blessed with this name and changed it into a symbol.

Vikram-Vetāla Relationship

Vetāla tested Vikram well before being ready to allow the dead body to be carried out; before exposing the wicked Monk; and before deciding to save him from being sacrificed and helping him in getting all the benefits of the sacrifices and penance that brought him under the control of the blessed king Vikramāditya. This was the beginning of Vikram-Vetāla Relationship.

With the help of Bhatti (This name has not been mentioned in this book *Vetāla Panchvinshat*), his wise and courageous minister Vikramāditya performed many great feats. Bhatti envisioned a marvelous 32 steps throne for Vikramāditya that had one Putali (Magical Figurine/ Nymph) made up of wood on each step. Vetāla created it. Vikramāditya sat on this high throne and passed orders. These came to light during the reign of Emperor Bhoja, when the throne was excavated and Bhoja tried to ascend it. The Figurines stopped him, saying that if you possess ten or even one percent of the wisdom and valour of Emperor Vikramāditya you can ascend the throne. Everyday, one Figurine narrated some great feats of the Trio: Vikramāditya-Vetāla and Bhatti. These tales have been collected in *Singhāsanvatishi.* That book throws ample light on Vikram-Vetāla Relationship that continued for a long time.

Balancing Act

It is here that one must advocate the need to maintain **balance**: from balanced thinking to balanced working; balance in production; balance in purchase; balance in distribution; balance in marketing; balance in the selection of work force; balance in the implementation of decisions.

Even If balance is maintained dangers can still be there; but those dangers will not affect the organisation either its functioning; growth; expenses or income as the organs will remain vital to write more success stories.

The Reversal

One may face reversals in life. But they are neither rare nor courteous. Reversals can spell doom but can be countered with innovations and rejuvenation. Resurgent energy is unbelievably powerful. A fallen King when rises conquers 'all'.

Reversals are not final defeat. Defeat is established when it is accepted. Genuine courage, confidence and willpower are needed to change reversals into profitable gains. One must be determined enough to declare, 'come what may, success will be mine!'

Management and these Stories

Management Related Stories

A cursory glance or a superfluous analysis may not connect these two highly popular figures of Ancient India to Modern Management of different organisations: business; social or government; national or international.

Management never means management of an organization or that of an office; it covers a vast field. The term management includes managing individuals, general public; distributing work; dividing them to subgroups; collection and distribution of information, resources and products; arranging money and streamlining payments for receipts and payments; collecting orders and creating opportunities and opening new vistas or repairing the recent as well remote losses and injuries. It may also include managing families and societies; departments, districts, divisions of government, parties, trade, shops, organizations, production and distribution units, of states or countries or international institutions.

Still the scope of Management is much more; those that are well defined and explained in books and those still not touched upon seriously. Yet, something unforeseen and unexpected crops up, they are taken as part of crisis management. In short, it is the management of life and its different organs and activities.

Vikram and Vetāla tackle unusual problems in unusual ways; and clarify the situation and problems. Apparently they seem to be unrelated to management but the stories are such that they are told in a fashion to cover different aspects of life and provide well-defined solutions. They raise very technical problems and present crystal clear solutions. Special care has been taken to explain them well in the context of management in a helpful way in each of the steps.

Facets of Management

Management begins with self-management. Then, it imperceptibly switches over to time-management and to family management covering management of family members and family needs. Those who have learnt it keep an eye on virtually everything with amazing ease and clarity can derive immense success by growing well, bearing burden, doing justice to responsibilities, fulfilling duties, and acquiring experience showing learning, labour, skill and ability.

It makes no difference whether they secure a job or enter a profession or start an independent organization, they are successful everywhere for they know how to manage money, material and man; the production or purchase and the distribution or marketing.

They are the most successful and happy men who achieve a balance in all fields – from self-management to market-management. Their gross income may not be very high but their net profit is always high and keeps them happy. Those who go all out for money get money but lose health and happiness and hence miss out on the essence of life.

Extravagant persons invite bankruptcy; miserly invite dislike and disdain; but the frugal, the economical maintain a balance between income and expenditure, live well, and are liked and loved by all. And, only they can manage an organisation well – local or international.

Vikram's Insight into Vetāla Management

Vikram's Insight into Vetāla Management is based on the famous storybook in Sanskrit called *"Vetālapanchvinshati"* that has two main characters: a Vetāla and the Emperor Vikram. In this book, the Vetāla represents the Organization and poses numerous problems that are to be solved by Vikram who represents the management and offers correct solutions in a distinct way. If Vikram fails, his head will splinter into pieces; if the Management fails the organization will scatter and perish. If Vikram as the management succeeds, the organisation will give him absolute power and super prosperity.

The book brings out the inner workings; intricacies; important points of management to the surface through Vetala's famous tales as told to Vikram and provides the most appropriate analysis by explaining Vikram's answers in the context of modern day management that too in a global perspective.

The tales have been told in their original form and format but illuminated, illustrated and elucidated in the new, changed and modern context. It is all for the benefit of executives and would be executives; and definitely suits the current scenario, needs and mood of the 21st Millennium; national, international markets, organizations and management. Based on the experiences from the past, this book can remain useful for the present and future. Naturally, it will work as a textbook, reference book and personal guide.

Diversity Rules in Management

Diversity is all encompassing; life, living conditions, availability of materials, know-how, technology, skills and finish; and above all diversity in thinking. This is because Nature by itself is heterogeneous and combines diverse elements and materials; working patterns and cultural affiliations; human whims and Nature's terror; and in between human fallacies and inhuman behaviour.

Thus diversity constitutes the underlying factor of management. There are many intricacies to be taken care of in order to successfully run an organization. Ranging from the managing of resources to ensuring decent profit, many centralised and decentralised factors are to be judged and handled delicately. Only then, discipline can be maintained and smooth functioning ensured; credibility sustains and the organisations move into the desired track. The ways are difficult; ifs and buts numerous; no-wind and hurricane zones immense to be crossed safely time to achieve immediate as well as distant goals. The bottom line is that it has to be done within the organization using the available work force, infrastructure, machinery, products and purchases amidst uncertainties in the market.

For Vikram, the immediate goal was to bring Vetāla to the designated place. In the difficult circumstances Vikram had to travel, fight clumsy situations and return to the same point to restart the exercise all over again.

Patience and Persistence

Thus any journey to the top calls for patience and persistence. None can be catapulted to the top in a day or two. Good management takes care of steady rise over a period of time. But those who run fast will lose breath and collapse. It is a fact that organizations come and go; but only the well managed will survive.

We do hear stories that hard work and consistent labour put in by men for decades being ignored or invariably set aside. It is important to organise and raise an organization first. As in the case of human life which starts with conception and delivery; fostering and education; the journey is filled with both pleasure and pain until the baby stands erect as a mature person. It is true that the baby did not become so in a fine morning at its 25th year. He grew for more than twenty-five years. The parents (particularly, the mother) prepared themselves for many years before that conception or delivery. So behind the success of any organization there is always an unaccounted period of preparedness that needs to be recognized. If that is so then the young people will not be misled by the European slogan that 'life has become very fast'. Only vehicles are running fast, life is moving on its natural pace dictated and controlled by time. One month does not pass in a week or a year is not passing in a month. It still takes 365 days to complete a year, and 18 years to get voting right.

If Vikram's Insight in Vetāla Management is followed well, in reading, understanding, imbibing and implementing; then success will never be a problem. Vetāla will remain under control and the final outcome will be 'bliss and blessing'.

Introduction is being concluded with an advice to all:

> ➤ Periodical cleaning is better than total renovation.
> ➤ Denotation is as important as subjective connotation.
> ➤ They are the most successful executives who are Equally driven by both tradition and innovation.

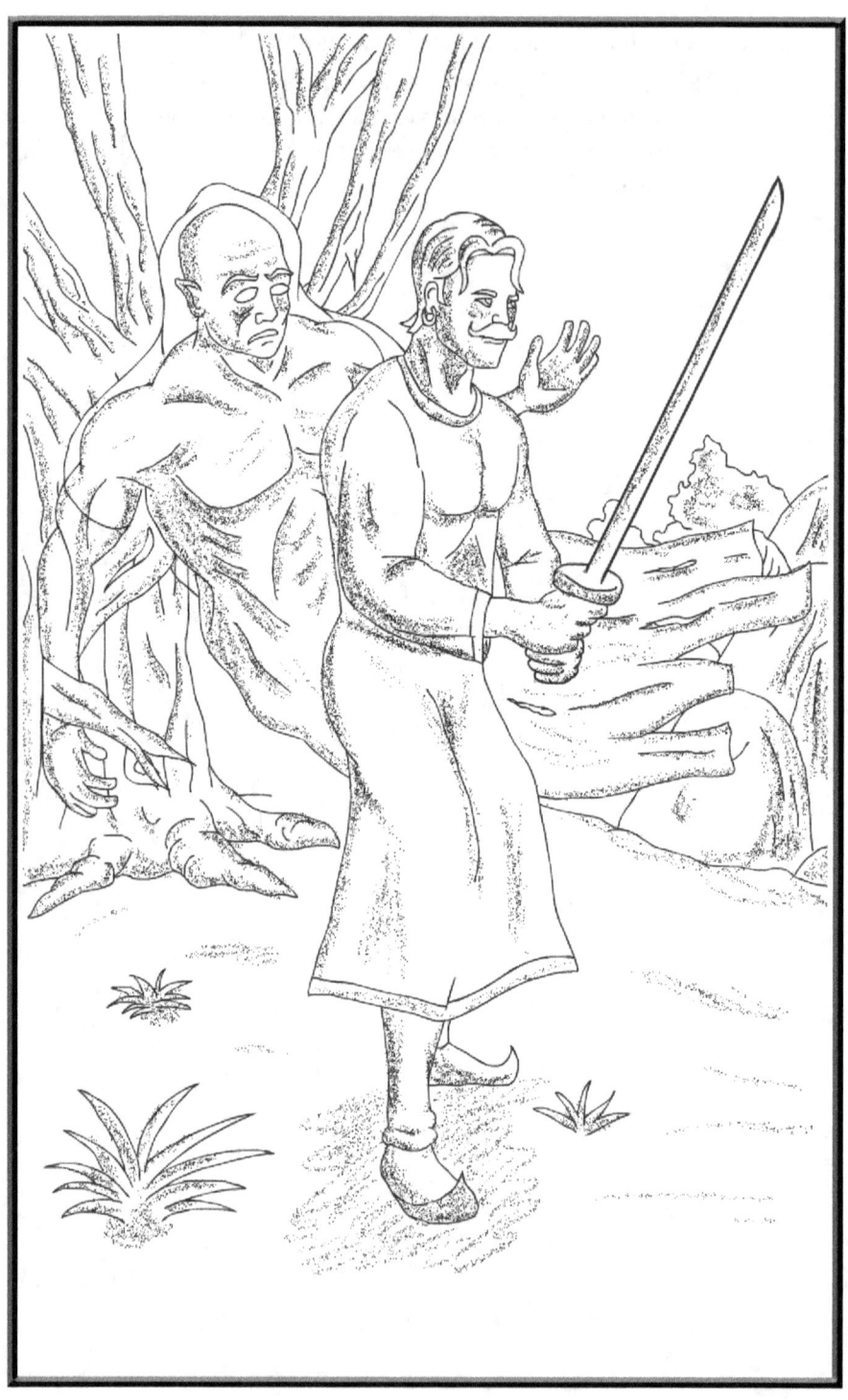

Prologue

Vikram Comes to Burning Ghāta

There was a country called Pratishthāna on the bank of River Godāvari ruled by a very strong, famous and virtuous king known as Trivikramasena, who was the son of king Vikramasena.

A Buddha Monk named Kshāntisheela came to the palace and used to offer a fruit to the King while attending the court. Every day the king would pass on the fruit to his treasurer, standing by him.

This way twelve long years passed. One day, the Buddha Monk gave the king a fruit and returned from the court. It was just a chance that the king gave the fruit to a little monkey that had stealthily entered the court along with the guards. When the little monkey bit the fruit, a rare jewel fell from it. The king picked it up and asked the treasurer, "Where have you stored all the fruits given by the Buddha Monk, which I had passed on to you?" The Treasurer was shocked at the question and feared punishment. He politely said, "As a habit I used to drop the fruits inside the Treasure House through a window. If you permit me, I would go and search them there."

The king granted permission. The Treasurer went to check it and soon returned and said, "O King! All the rotten fruits are lying there but rays of bright jewels are coming from them." The king was satisfied. He ordered the Treasurer to clean the area and keep the jewels safe.

Next day, when the Monk came to the court and offered the fruit to the king, he refused to take it and asked, "Why do you give me such costly gifts? What is your intention? What do you want? I won't accept your gift until I get a convincing answer from you."

The Monk said, "I can answer you and tell the purpose when no one is around." The King agreed. They went to a lonely place. Then the Monk said, "O Valiant King! A penance awaits your help. In that penance I need your brave help."

The king replied, "I'll help you." He gave his word to help the Monk. The Monk became happy with the assurance and told the king, "In the beginning of the 14th day of the next moonless fortnight come to the biggest crematorium or burning *ghāta*. I will be sitting there under a big banyan tree. We can meet"

The king said, "Okay, I'll be there."

The pleased Monk Kshāntisheel returned to his place.

On the fourteenth day of the next moonless fortnight, the valiant king got ready to keep his word given to the Monk. The king covered his head with a blue cloth; took out the sharpest, shining sword and went towards the biggest burning *ghāta* in disguise to avoid anybody recognizing him. The King found the Monk sitting under the big banyan tree and chanting *Mantras*. He went closer to the Monk and said, "O Monk! I have come. Tell me, what should I do now?"

The Monk was pleased to see the king. He said happily, "If you're kind enough, then please go alone in the southern direction. At a distance, you'll find a dead body hanging by a *sheesham* (the Indian rosewood) tree. Bring that dead body here and help me."

Unfazed, the valiant king, true to his promise, said, "Okay!" and proceeded to the south. Moving south through the burning *ghāta*, somehow he reached the rosewood tree and found a dead body hanging up on its branch. He climbed the tree, cut the rope and the dead body fell on the earth with a thud. The moment the dead body hit the ground it started weeping like a living creature under great pain caused by the hard fall.

The king climbed down. Thinking the body to be alive, he touched it. The moment, the King touched the body, the corpse started laughing. The King felt some ghostly spirit had possessed the body. He questioned, "Why are you laughing?" and commanded, "Let us move."

The fearless King Vikram bent towards the corpse to lift it and lo, it was nowhere!. The King looked up and saw the corpse hanging in the same branch as it was before. The King again climbed up the tree cautiously and brought it again.

Lifting the corpse up to his shoulder, the King started walking back towards the Monk. By this time Vetāla had taken its seat on the dead body; Vetāla said, "O Emperor! I will tell you a story to entertain you on the way. Now, listen."

Do not poke nose into matters pertaining to others if it is not so

courage, credit and reputation.

'Persistence and diligence are virtues that lead to success.'

1

Prince Vajramukuta and Padmāwati

The city of Varanasi is the abode of Lord Shri Shankar. Only gentlemen inhabit the city as Kailāsh is protected by the *Yakshaa* and Spirits. The Ganges beautifies it as a pearl-garland.

In the Varanasi city, reigned a sublime emperor named Pratapmukuta. The King had a valiant son named Vajramukuta whose close friend and adviser was the son of the learned Minister.

One day, the prince went on a hunting expedition with his friend and reached a dense forest. The tired duo found a reservoir where they cleaned their hands and feet, drank clean water, and sat under the shade of a tree to take rest.

In the meantime, there arrived a beautiful damsel in costly clothes to take bath and filled the reservoir with her splendid beauty. In a single glance, the prince lost his heart to that lady. Passion welled up in the beautiful girl too, who could not speak because she was too shy. She conveyed her desire in the tough language of sign by placing a lotus on her ears and touching her teeth with it. She placed the lotus first on her head then on the breasts. The prince failed to understand the meaning of her strange actions. But the wise minister's son understood the secret signals from the girl.

After a while, the girl returned accompanied by her maids. At home, she fell flat on the bed by immersing herself in the memory of the prince. The prince too returned and became morose at the thoughts of that beautiful lady. He grew weak as he could not shake off the charming girl's portrait from the mind.

However, the prince was pacified by his friend who worked out a ruse to meet up with the girl. The duo secretly made a plan and went hunting again, only to meet that charming lady. They reached the reservoir. Since they galloped the horses fast, soldiers and the servants were left far behind.

The Prince and friend came to Kaling, the country of King Karnotapala. There they found out the residence of the dentist Sangramvardhan and also located a suitable house nearby for themselves. It belonged to a poor old woman.

They asked the old woman, "Do you know a dentist living here?' She replied in the affirmative and added, "I serve his dear daughter Padmāwati". The minister's son gave his *dupattā* (a big scarf) to the old woman and said, "O Mother! Go to that lady and tell her as we tell you. Do it very secretly. Go to Padmāwati, the daughter of the Dentist, and say that the prince whom she met near the reservoir has come here. On his request I have come to inform you of his love."

The old lady obliged them and immediately headed to the dentist's house and talked to Padmāwati. The old woman told her:, "O dear child! Those two men, the Prince and the minister's son have come for you. What do you have to say?"

Padmāwati bristled in anger and chided the old lady for the errand. She then smeared camphor on her hands and slapped the old lady. The imprints of all her ten fingers stood visible on the cheeks of the old woman. Aggrieved at the insult she returned and said, "She only gave them." The prince was shocked at the insult. But his wise friend took it differently and told the prince, "O Prince! Don't be aggrieved on what has happened. It is exactly the answer to your enquiry. She has secretly sent the reply. She used camphor and slapped her printing the ten fingers. That means, the next ten moonlit nights are not suitable for meeting. So wait for the opportune moment."

This way he consoled the Prince. The Prince became happy. They secretly sold a costly wristband in the market and gave enough money to the old lady to prepare delicious meals of royal quality for them. They ate sumptuously and stayed there for the next ten days. When the ten forbidden days were over, the minister's son again sent that old woman to Padmāwati. As the old woman was satisfied with the sweet and delicious dishes that she got everyday; she agreed to go.

When she returned, said, "My sons! I went there and sat silently for a long time. She said that I have committed a crime by talking to you people. Then she dipped her three fingers in *āltā* (red coloured liquid for decorating feet) and hit me hard on my chest. You can see the impression made by the fingers. Again she insulted me and I returned, sadly and in agony."

The prince again felt sad about the insult. Again his wise friend intervened and told the Prince: "O Prince! Don't worry at what has

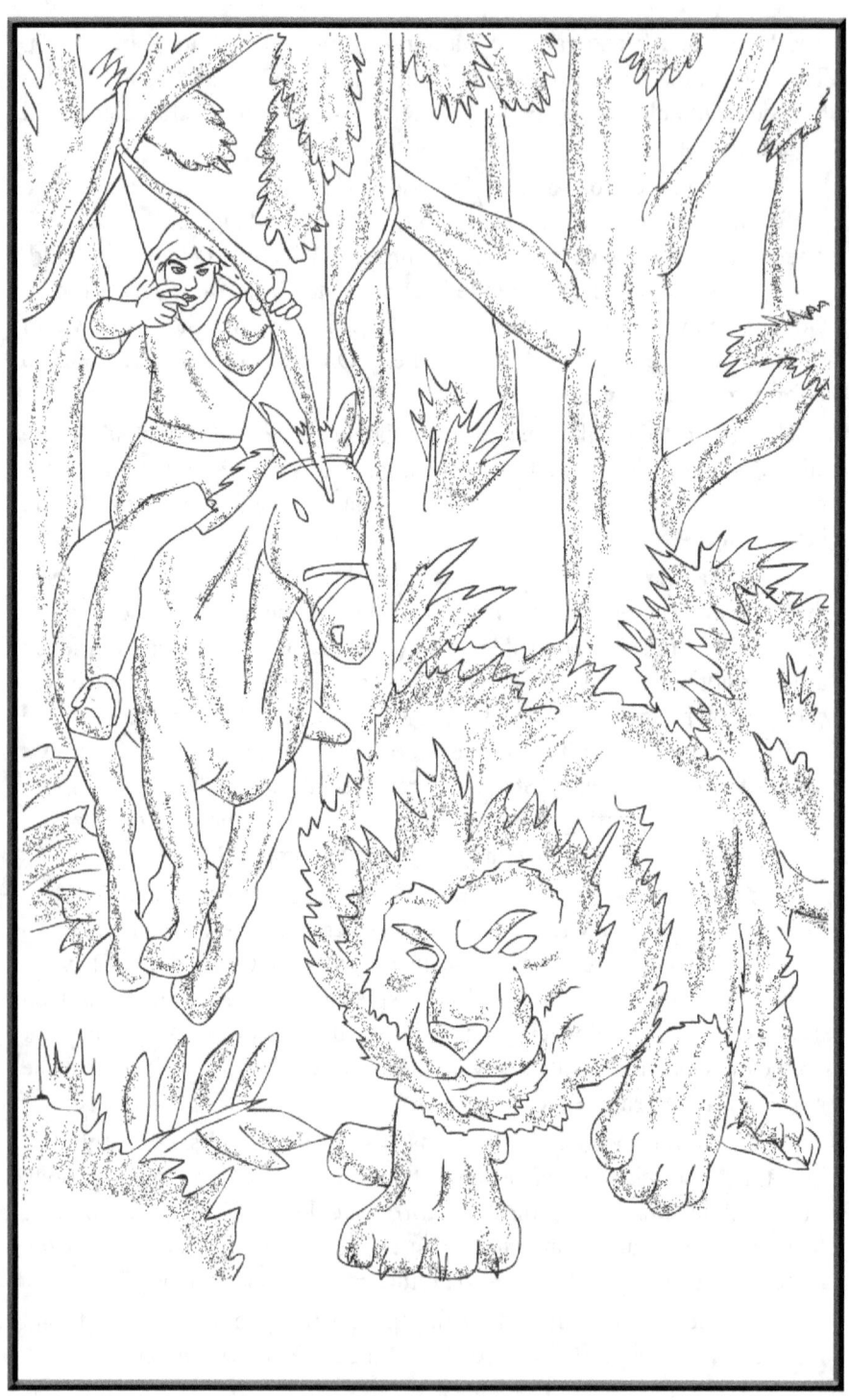

happened. It is the perfect answer to your query. The red colour she has used and the three fingers clearly indicate that she will be in her menstruation period for the next three days."

They stayed there for three more days. When the three forbidden days were over, the son of the minister again sent that old woman to Padmāwati. This time, she welcomed the old woman, gave her nice food and gifts; and she was entertained daylong.

In the evening when she wanted to return, there was a commotion outside as one elephant had gone mad. Padmāwati told the old woman, "O Mother! It's not safe to go through the main gate and main road. An elephant is running amok. She took her to a large window and asked her to sit on a pedestal. With the help of four ropes, she was dropped down into the backyard garden as promised. The old woman knew the tree. She climbed it and promptly got down the boundary wall, returned home, and narrated the whole incident to the Prince and his friend.

When they were alone, the minister's son said, "Congratulations friend! Your desires are about to be fulfilled. The night for the long awaited union has come. She has shown the way. So, you must go there this night itself". The Prince agreed. They reached the backyard garden.

The pedestal with ropes was hanging there as indicated by the secret message. The prince stood on the pedestal. It was pulled up, apparently, the maids of Padmāwati pulled it up. The prince went inside through a wide and large window. After this, the minister's son returned to his temporary abode.

The prince saw the glowing face of Padmāwati that was like a full moon. She also looked at him intensely with excited, scintillating eyes. They locked themselves in passionate embrace. Then the rituals of *gandharva vivāha* were performed and they became man and wife. The Prince secretly stayed lived with her for about a fortnight. One day, he said to Padmāwati, "Dear! My friend, the son of the minister has come with me. He is staying alone with that old woman. I wish to go to meet him and I promise to return."

Padmāwati said, "Who understood the secret signs that I made to send different messages, you or your friend?"

The innocent Prince said, "I could not understand even a bit. I was sad. It was my friend with extraordinary knowledge and presence of mind who deciphered them to me."

"Then my dear husband! I should have honoured him with betel and other offerings," mulled Padmāwati. With her permission, the Prince returned to his friend and told his friend what wife Padmawati said about him. The son of the minister said, "It's not ethical".

In the morning they got ready. In the meantime, one of the friends of Padmāwati came with rich and delicious food and betel and asked for the minister's son. But she dissuaded the Prince from taking the food, "Your beloved is waiting and expects you to take food with her." She expressed her request and returned.

The minister's son said: O Master! I will show you a play for fun. He called a dog and gave a portion of the food to it. The dog ate it and died instantly. At this, the Prince asked, "What is it? It's a wonder. What is the meaning?"

The minister's son replied, "O Master! I understood her secret messages. She feels that I'm wise and you're fixated with me. She suspects that any time you can turn towards me and return to the kingdom. That is why she decided to kill me by poisoning the food. You should not get angry with her. It is just a general psychology of anylady in love. Now I will plan things in a different way. See it". The Prince said, "It's true that you are an emblem of wisdom."

Suddenly, there was a commotion outside. They heard people weeping and saying, 'The King's youngest son died.' The minister's son was pleased to hear the tragic news and told the Prince, "O Master! Please go to Padmāwati, and lull her into drinking a lot of drugged juice till she falls flat like a dead body. Then, take this trident that I am giving you; heat it hard and when she is unconscious cauterize and make a mark near her navel. After that collect all her ornaments and come back here. I'm sure, everything will be all right." He took out a small trident and gave it to the Prince.

The Prince took the trident and left for Padmāwati's residence. He was determined to follow the instructions of his friend and make a mark on his beloved wife with the hot trident.

The Prince followed the instructions meticulously. When Padmāwati became unconscious the Prince branded near her navel with the tip of hot trident; collected her ornaments and left. After that, the Prince and friend left the place of the old woman and headed to the burning *ghāta* in disguise with the minister's son acting as as a saint in penance and the Prince as his disciple. When the make-up was complete, he checked the ornaments and selected a necklace of pearl. He gave it to the Prince and instructed, "Go and try to sell this necklace of pearls in the open market. When the guards of the city arrest you then say that you know nothing about the necklace; that your *guru* (preceptor) had given it to sell. You are obeying him. If they have some questions to ask they can come to the burning *ghāta* to question the guru."

The Prince did exactly what his friend had told him. While trying to sell the ornament he was arrested. The guards were looking for the thief who had stolen the ornaments of the dentist's daughter. They brought him to the Mayor of the city. The Mayor was surprised to see the man in the garb of an ascetic. He asked him gently, "Mahāshaya! (Sir) Where did you get this necklace of pearls? It's a part of the ornament stolen from the daughter of the dentist."

The Prince was bold; he said, "My guru has given me to sell it. You can come and ask him."

Then, they all came to the son of the minister who was sitting like a recluse. The Mayor asked, "From where did your disciple get this necklace?"

The minister's son called him aside and whispered cunningly, "Well, Gentleman! I move from place to place in this world. It's just a chance that I'm staying here in this burning *ghāta*. Last night, I saw the complete constellation of Yoginis (Female Ascetic Attendants). One of them broke open the heart of a Prince like a lotus flower and offered to Bhairava as sacrifice. She was full of pride and intoxicated to a great extent. She had many illusory and magical powers. Her face was deformed and she appeared wicked. When she tried to snatch my rosary I became angry and branded her near her navel with the tip of my trident heated by Mantras; and snatched off the necklace of pearl from her neck. But it's not worthy to be with an ascetic in penance, so I asked my disciple to sell it in the market."

The Mayor was satisfied with the answer and briefed the king. The king sent an old lady to verify the mark at the navel of Padmāwati. She confirmed the trident mark near her navel. Now, the king was sure that Padmāwati only killed his loving son. The King approached the minister's son under false penance and asked for a suitable punishment to Padmāwati. The guru ordained that she should be asked to leave the city and take shelter in a forest.

The order was passed and Padmāwati was exiled from the city. Padmāwati easily surmised that the wise son of the minister only planned it. Hence she did not commit suicide. As expected, the Prince and the friend came to her on a horse-back and took her to their kingdom safely. They spent their life happily thereafter.

But it was unbearable for the dentist. He believed that his dear daughter had been killed and devoured by wild animals in the forest. He died soon followed by his wife.

Indicating that the story was over, the Vetāla paused and later asked King Vikram, "O King! Who, among the Prince, the minister's son, Padmāwati is responsible for the murder of the innocent father and mother of Padmāwati? If you know the answer and do not tell the truth, your head will break into one hundred pieces; and if you give the correct answer then I would return to that rosewood tree."

The king answered, "None of the three persons you cited are responsible for the twin murders of innocent persons. Only the King Karnotapal is the sinner".

Vetāla asked, "Why blame the king? What is his offence?" Then the King said, "None of the three is at fault. It was the duty of the son of the minister to help his master, so he is innocent. Padmāwati and the Prince were in love, so, they were unable to think clearly. They were interested in their union. So, they are innocent. The King was well versed in moral, ethical and political teachings. He knew the cunningness of people. Yet he did not take the help of his secret agents. He did not try to understand the reality. He took his decision without reasoning and gave inadequate thought to the problem. So, he is the sinner."

Vetāla heard it and returned to the rosewood tree. Undaunted the King marched towards that rosewood tree to take him to the Monk.

In th

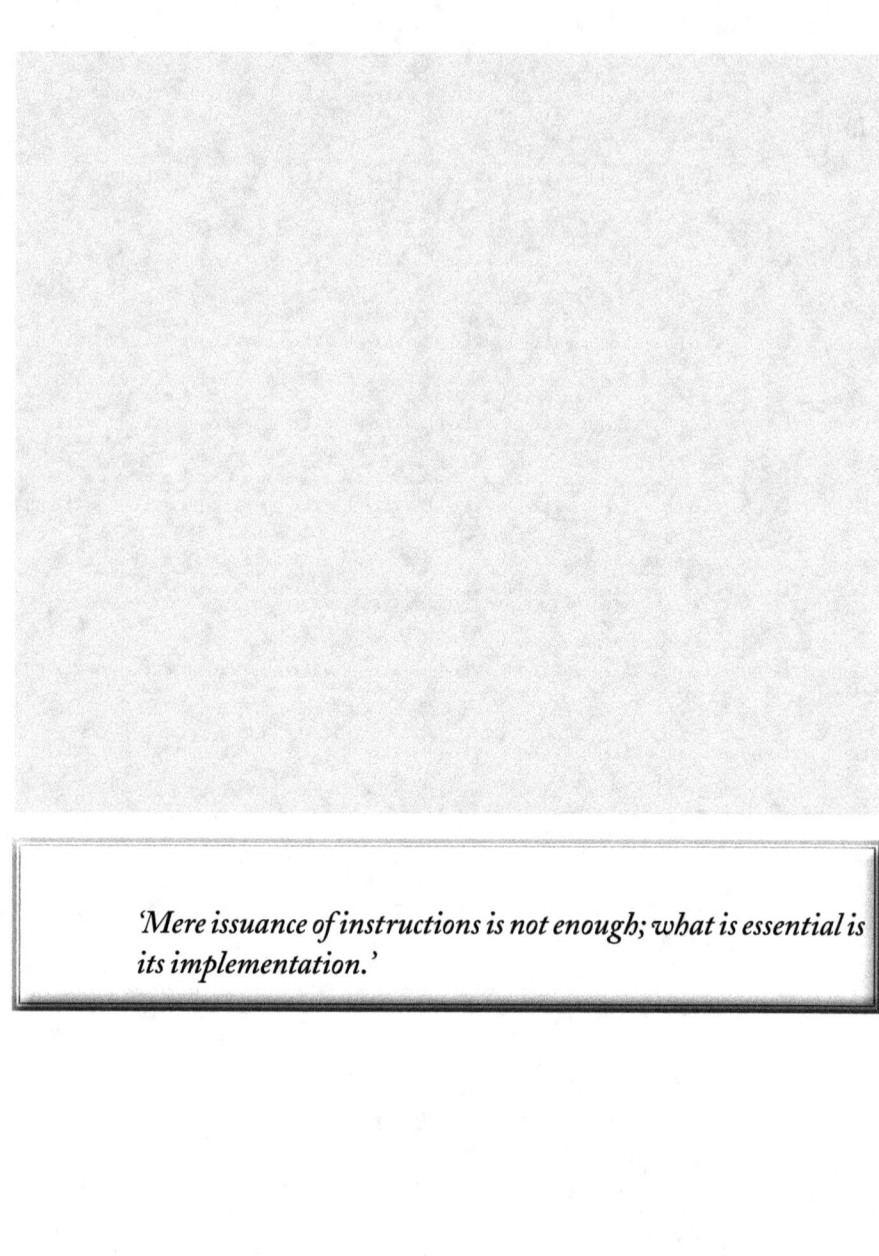

'Mere issuance of instructions is not enough; what is essential is its implementation.'

2

Gain is generally comparative and never superlative;
It should be ideally positive and surely productive;
Management links demand and fulfillment
And to maintain everything existing and creative

The Marriage of Mandārwati

Finishing his story, the Vetāla retreated to the rosewood tree and King Trivikram Sen with greater resolve approached the rosewood tree again. Not finding Vetāla there, he looked around and saw Vetāla lying on the ground and telling something inaudible.

The King lifted the dead body to his shoulder and started moving hastily. The Vetāla said, "O Emperor! You have fallen in unwarranted pain; so, for your entertainment I may tell you a story. Now listen."

There was a village named Brahmasthal on the bank of the holy river Yamuna. There lived Agniswami, a Brahmin who was an expert in Vedic Knowledge and had a beautiful daughter named Mandārwati.

On attaining puberty, Mandarwati started getting marriage proposals. One day three young, handsome, learned Brahmin youth of qualities approached her father seeking the hand of Mandārwati in marriage. Her father thought, 'I won't have to search for anyone else. I'll select one of these three for my daughter.'

However, cleaver Mandārwati understood that her marriage to one of them would emotionally hurt the other two. So she postponed her marriage. Like a *Chakore* bird, all the three Brahmins were looking at the moonlike face of that extremely beautiful girl Mandārwati all the time.

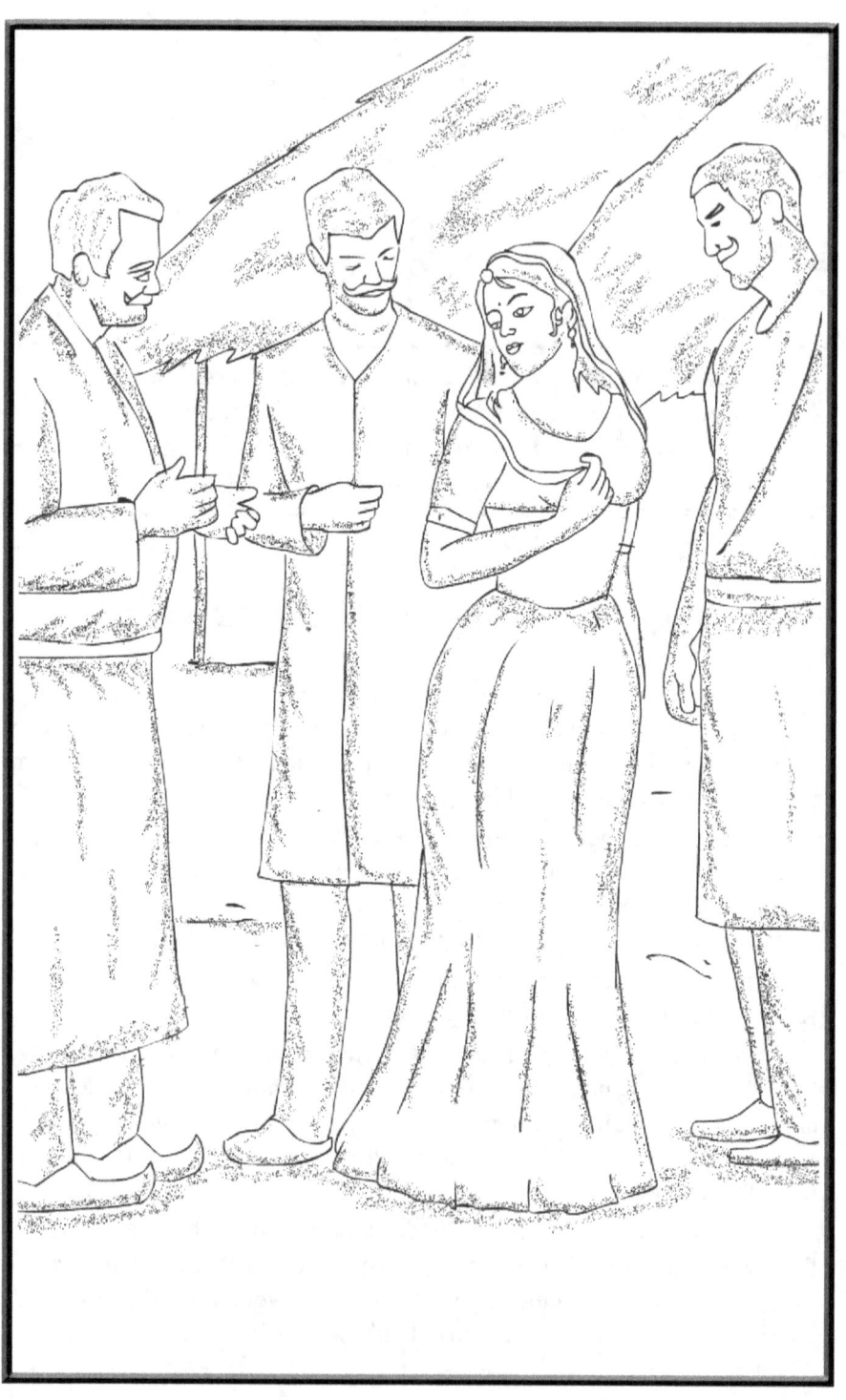

But tragedy struck; Mandārwati died of sudden illness. The three Brahmin youth plunged into unbearable grief. The grief-laden Brahmin youth decorated her dead body with ornaments and flowers; carried it to the burning *ghāta*; placed it on the pyre and completed the last rites.

One of them even erected a hut at the crematorium and made a bed of her ashes and started living on it munching her memories and lived on alms from begging. The second Brahmin immersed her bones in the Ganges for her purgation and salvation. The third Brahmin went on a pilgrimage and turned an ascetic. He moved from place to place ostensibly to shake off her memories.

One day he was staying at another Brahmin's house. The family called him for dinner. When dinner was ready one of the sons of the Brahmin started crying. Despite his mother's efforts the boy kept crying in a loud voice. In a fit of anger, the Brahmin's wife threw the boy into the fire and the tender child instantly burnt to death. For the Brahmin youth, it was an unbearable sight. He rose in anger and yelled at them, calling them "murderers" and announced, "I entered the house of a demon. Obviously, the grains of the place are sinful. So I wouldn't take your meal."

The host tried to pacify him, saying, "Oh, Brahmin, it is not the way you think it is. See, you must see the power of learned men." Saying thus, he opened a book and started chanting the *Mantras* and sprinkled water on the fire where his son was gutted. A miracle happened—the boy came alive from the fire. The ascetic happily had his food. The host Brahmin kept the book in a bag and hung it by a peg and slept.

But Brahmin youth was restless. In the night, the young Brahmin got up, grabbed the important book and ran away hoping that he can restore the life of Mandārwati. After a hazardous journey, he did reach the burning *ghāta* where he met the other two Brahmin youth. The second one, who had gone to offer immerse the bones at the Ganges had also returned.

The young Brahmin with the magical book told the one who was living in a hut of Mandārwati's ashes, "O Brother! Leave this hut. I will give life to that beloved." The young Brahmin opened the book and started chanting the *Mantra*. Thereafter he sprinkled divine water on the ashes of Mandārwati. To everyone's surprise, Mandārwati came to life again; bowed to all; saluted the Fire god; and came out with the golden hue of the fire adding more glow to her beauty.

The love flashed again and the three Brahmin youth started fighting on their respective claims to marry her. One said, "She came to life with the effect of my *Mantras*, so I have the right to marry her."

The second one retorted, "She came to life because I visited, and prayed at many pilgrim centres and accumulated virtues."

The one who remained at the burning *ghāta* exclaimed, "I kept her ashes safe. That is why she came to life again. Without the ashes, how could have been that possible. So, I only have the right to marry her."

Vetāla went mum for a moment indicating the end of the story. After a short pause, he said, "O Emperor! Now say, whose wife should the girl be? If you knowingly tell a lie your head will go into splinters."

King Vikram heard it patiently and analysed it wisely, then said, "One of the Brahmin youth did the duty of a father by bringing the *Mantras* that gave her life. He cannot be a husband. The other did the work of a son by immersing the bones and ashes at the Ganges. He too cannot be a husband. So, the only one who behaved like a true lover and lived on her ashes at the burning *ghāta* qualifiy to be her husband."

Vetāla heard King Vikram intently and left the moment the king completed the answer and retreated to the rosewood tree. The king decided to fetch him again for the Monk. Great people never quit their mission without accomplishing the goals despite challenges. They leave no task unfinished.

any organisation.

The three Brahmin youth can be compared to modern day

on percentage basis.

better than many others. There must be better reasoning behind

3

The Parrot and Mynah

King Vikramaditya again went to the mysterious rosewood tree and lifted the dead body possessed by Vetāla. Raising the corpse on his shoulders, the King started walking briskly but silently towards the Buddha Monk.

As usual, Vetāla broke his silence and told the king, "Oh Emperor! While walking in the night you might be facing many hurdles. So, for entertainment I am going to tell you a story. Please, listen to it attentively."

In the ancient period, there was a famous city called Pātaliputra ruled by Emperor Vikramakeshari. The King had a treasure of jewels and jewel-like qualities. He also had a unique Parrot, which knew all the classics and scriptures. It was a curse that made it to take birth as a Parrot.

Shashi—the emperor's son married Princess Chandraprabhā, the daughter of the king of Magadh, on the advice of the Parrot. The Princess had a Mynah called Somikā which was as wise as the Parrot. After the marriage both the Parrot and the Mynah were put into a single cage and they lived together.

One day, out of severe passion, the Parrot told the Mynah, "O Beauty! Please sleep with me in on one bed; sit on one pedestal; take meal and enjoy life together." The Mynah said, "I don't like contact with any males as they

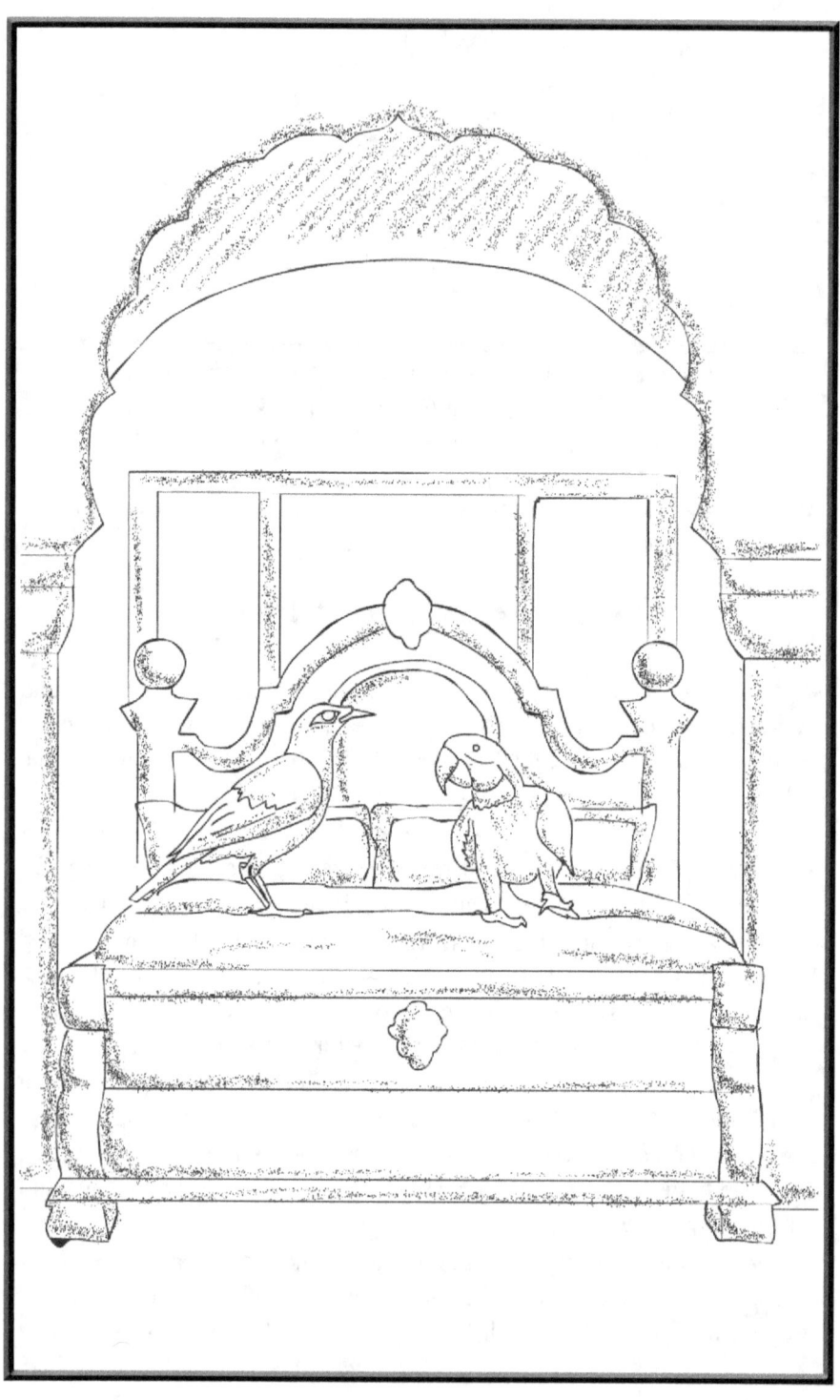

are wicked and ungrateful." Then, the Parrot said, "Males are not wicked, females are wicked and very cruel at heart."

Finally they entered into a bet on the condition that the defeated party would serve as the slave of the other. To resolve the issue, they approached the Prince sitting at the palace court. The Prince heard them asked Mynah to establish as to how the males are wicked and ungrateful?

Mynah started a story to justify her statement that males are wicked and ungrateful.

"In the famous city of Kāmandaki, lived a wealthy merchant Arthadatta. After some time, he had a son named Dhanadatta. After the demise of his father, the young son wasted his wealth on gambling. He kept company with the wicked and evil people. Finally he exhausted all assets and became penniless. Finding it difficult to live as a loser among the people who know him, Dhanadatta left his country and took shelter in another country.

At Chandanpur, he met a merchant who offered him food. The merchant understood that his guest was a bachelor and enquired about his whereabouts. He assumed that his guest belonged to a high family. The merchant decided to marry off his daughter Ratnawati with the young man and gave her lots of wealth and precious ornaments during the marriage. Even after marriage, Dhandatta continued living in the house of his father-in-law. In the new life of luxury, he forgot his penurious condition and old habits started beckoning him again. He longed for the company of gamblers friends and decided to return to his country. He requested his father-in-law to allow him to go, who reluctantly agreed.

He also took wife Ratnawati along with her ornaments and jewels. Her father sent an old lady to accompany his daughter in the journey to her husband's native place. As soon as they entered a jungle, Dhanadatta had his despicable ways; on the pretext of keeping her ornaments and jewels in safe custody from the robbers, he cleverly snatched her jewels.

The Mynah continued, "That sinner blinded by his greed for wealth, then threw his wife and the old woman into a deep ditch. The seriously injured old lady died and Ratnawati, somehow escaped with the help of grass creepers and came out. Retracing her path after making queries to the passers by, she somehow returned to her parents' place.

Seeing Ratnavati in a pitiful condition, her father was in pain and wonder. He asked, "How and why did you come back so soon and in such a miserable condition?"

Ratnavati, a loyal wife, narrated the happenings differently. She said, "On the way thieves robbed us; kidnapped my husband; the old lady fell into a ditch and died. By God's grace, I survived. With the help of some travellers I pulled myself out of the ditch and returned to you." The aggrieved parents consoled Ratnawati. She continued to live with her parents adjusting with what fate had given to her.

Time passed. Dhanatta again lost everything to gambling. When everything was over, he thought, 'Why not go back to father-in-law and bring more wealth. I must tell him that his daughter is with me at home.' With a diabolic plan he headed to his father-in-law's house. His wife saw him from a distance and ran towards him. He was surprised to see her. She fell on his feet, narrated what she had told her parents to salvage his honour. Ratnawati pleaded him not to ditch her.

Despite the wickedness of husbands sincere wives do not deviate from virtuous ways. The wicked son-in-law entered the house again, touched the feet of father-in-law who was pleased to see him back. He welcomed him, "It is just good luck that the thieves released my son-in-law unhurt." He even arranged a grand feast to celebrate the reunion. Wicked Dhandatta happily lived some more time on the earnings and wealth of his father-in-law and enjoyed life further.

One night, wicked Dhandatta killed his faithful wife who was sleeping and stashed away all her jewels and ornaments and fled the country. "This way, it is very clear that the males are sinners and most ungrateful", the Mynah quipped.

After the Mynah's turn, the Prince asked the Parrot to present his version. Then the Parrot said, "Females are cruel hearted, adventurous, indulge in misconduct and are sinners. I'm telling such a tale. O Prince! Listen!

There was a city named Harshwati where a multibillionaire merchant called Dharmadatta lived.

His beautiful daughter was Basudattā whom he loved more than his life. The merchant married off his daughter to Samudradatta, who was the son of another merchant in Tāmralipta.

One day, when her husband was with his parents at his city, Basudattā chanced to see a handsome man from a distance. She sent her friend to invite him; enchanted him and made love with him. This way, this married woman enjoyed physical pleasure with that young man secretly.

One day, her husband was in town and the day was spent on festivities. At night, her mother dressed up Basudattā seductively and sent her to her husband's chamber. But she decided to avoid her husband's advances for copulation because she had only the secret lover in mind. On some excuse she denied him that conjugal pleasure and pretended very sleepy at the bed. The tired husband too fell asleep under intoxication. When everyone was fast asleep, a thief had intruded into the house for stealing ornaments. Bāsudattā did not see the thief. As usual, she got up from the bed and went out to meet her paramour.

Obviously, Basudattā was wearing many ornaments that night. The thief followed her stealthily, thinking, "Where is she going? She is going out in the wee hours. What will she do?" Keeping reasonable distance he followed her. She entered a nearby garden and went to the secret place but her secret lover was already killed. Mistaken for a thief, the paramour was caught and hanged by the city guards. Unable to bear the grief and sudden change in plans she fell on the ground and started weeping.

After a while, she brought down the hanging corpse of her paramour to the ground and decked it up with flowers. Her passions grew; she started kissing the dead body. In the meantime, a ghost also entered the dead body that cut her nose off. Reeling under pain, she started running away looking back at the corpse. She was confused, came back and again confirmed whether he was dead or alive. Again she wept and returned.

Now, Basudattā had to explain as on what circumstances the nose got cut off? She hatched a plan and as soon as she was near her husband, she started crying aloud. She screamed, "O! Help me! Save me from this butcher! This wicked husband is my enemy. He has cut off my nose."

Hearing her bitter cry all rushed to her room. The husband also woke up. But he could not make out the head or tail of what had happened. He knew nothing. Meanwhile, the thief escaped safely.

Basudattā's father was shivering with anger for the dastardly act of his son-in-law. He ordered the servants to immediately tie up the son-in-law with a rope. It was done. The next morning, the young husband was produced before the court of the king. Basudattā too came. The King was given a false account of all that never happened. The King came to the conclusion that the nose-chopping was done by the husband only and gave him death sentence.

When the sentence was being pronounced to the accompaniment of drumbeats and the 'culprit' was being led to the place of execution, the thief heard it all. Immediately the thief went straight to the King and presented the truth of all that took place in that fateful night. At the end he beseeched,

"O King! If you doubt my words, then the part of the nose should be verified in the mouth of the dead body."

Place Guards were deputed to verify it and found it true. Understanding his mistake King freed the husband. As a punishment, both ears of Basudattā were chopped and she was exiled from the country. Her father's property was also confiscated. Impressed by the truthfulness of the thief, the King appointed the thief as the Mayor of the city.

The Parrot paused for a second and concluded, "O Prince! See how women are cruel and low in morality."

The moment he finished it, the Parrot metamorphosed into *Chitraratha*, the king of Gandharvas, the celestial musicians. The period of his curse was over. A heavenly chariot descended; he boarded it and went towards heaven. The Mynah too became a nymph named Tillottamā and liberated from the curse. She flew up into the air. But their puzzle was still not resolved in that court of the Prince.

Vetāla finished the story and paused for a few seconds, then asked, "O Learned King! Please tell; who are the greater sinners – males or females? If you knowingly evade the answer your head will break up into pieces."

Vikram heard the Vetāla, and said, "Vetāla, there may be cases of men who were lustful; do gambling and torture wife but usually women are heard to be more sinning." The King finished his reply and the Vetāla vanished from his shoulder. Undaunted, the King returned to the rosewood tree again to take Vetāla to the Monk.

Gender mix in work force

most men in top positions. In these changing times, educating managers on management is a must.

'Leadership is interpersonal infl uence that motivates others to give their best to achieve known goals.'

4

Shudrak and Birwar

King Vikram slowly and steadily reached the rosewood tree and picked up the corpse, in which the laughing Vetāla resided. The King put the corpse onto his shoulder and started his fearless journey in darkness towards the Buddha Monk.

Sitting on the shoulders of King Vikram, Vetala said: "O Emperor! Why are you giving so much of importance to that wicked recluse? I don't see any wisdom in this useless effort. But I am pleased at your devotion. So, I am telling another story to keep off your tiredness from hard labour."

There was a beautiful city named Shobhāwati, which was ruled by a valiant king Shudrak who was the embodiment of many noble qualities that the people of his city even forgot the name of other great kings like Rama. He was such a perfect King and a noble ruler.

Once, a Kshatriya named Birwar, from Mālava, came to serve this king. His family included wife Dharmawati; son Shaktidhar and daughter Birwati. Birwar carried only three things as weapons for service – a dagger at the waist; a sword in one hand and a shield in the other. Despite the limited armoury; he demanded a hefty salary of five hundred gold coins every day.

Impressed by his appearance and valiant looks, the king accepted his demand. Out of curiosity, the King verified how he spent that money.

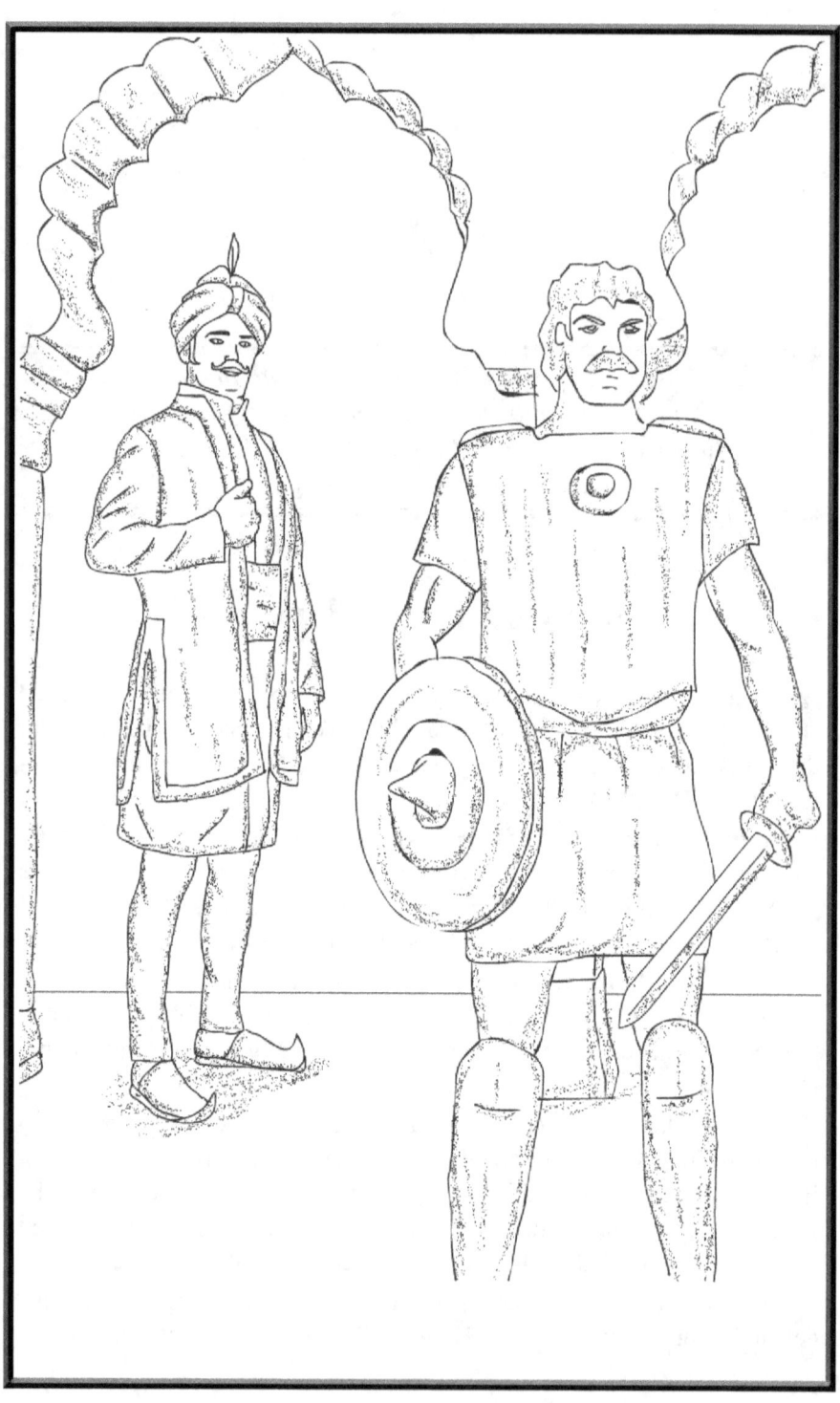

So the King asked his *guptchars* (the secret agents) to collect the relevant information. Every day he would spend the five hundred gold coins that he gets from the king in a very interesting way. He would give one hundred gold coins to his wife for domestic expenses; another one hundred goes for clothing, decorative articles, betel, etc; he would spend hundred more while worshipping Lord Vishnu and Lord Shiva. The balance two hundred was spent on charity – one hundred to Brahmins and another one hundred to the poor. In this way, he would spend all the five hundred gold coins every day.

Meeting the king was the first thing that Birwar would do in the morning and in the noon he would be guard the main gate standing in attention.

After completing everything, he would go to the main gate during the night and stand as a guard with the naked sword in hand.

The king was satisfied and valued Birwar as someone very special. Months passed. One night it was raining heavily and all the roads were empty; Birwar was guarding the main gate. When the night fell and darkness spread, the King, decided to test the sincerity and faithfulness of Birwar, went up to the palace and asked, "Who is guarding the Singhdwār (main gate)?

"It is I, Birwar." Birwar answered. The King was pleased and appreciated his devotion to the job and thought he deserved a higher post and greater responsibility.

The rains continued for the second night also. The drizzle had already become a torrent. Because of rainy clouds, darkness engulfed everywhere. The King, again decided to test his sincerity and faithfulness; went up the palace and asked, "Who is guarding the main gate? "It is I, Birwar." Birwar answered. When the pleased King was about to return, he heard the painful cries of a woman.

Out of kindness and compassion, the King ordered Birwar, "O Birwar! Listen! Someone is weeping somewhere. Who is she and why is she weeping? Go, and investigate".

Birwar said, "O King! As you wish"! Saying this, Birwar headed to the direction of the cries. Birwar had a dagger at the waist and open sword in the hand. Neither heavy rains nor hailstorm in that darkness stopped him. The King also got curious. He too reached the main gate and charged ahead with an open sword. The King followed Birwar stealthily without being noticed.

Birwar moved into a certain direction and came out of the city and reached the vicinity of a big reservoir where he heard the cries nearby: "O

Warrior! O Kind! O Charitable! How will I live without you?" Birwar saw a lady standing in the water of the reservoir. He asked, "Who are you? Why are you weeping?"

She said, "O Birwar! You can take me to be the earth (Prithvi). The most religious king of the earth (Prithvipati) is King Shudrak. He is like my husband. He will die on the third day. Then, how will I get such a husband? I'm weeping out of that pain while thinking of the days after his death. Fear ran through his spinal cord. He patiently asked, "O Devi! Is there any way out? How can the king be saved?"

Then, the earth answered, "O Son! There is only one way and you can do it." Birwar said impatiently, "Then, tell me fast, so that the right steps can be immediately taken. Otherwise, what is the use of my life?"

The earth said, "Listen to the relief. There is a temple of Chandikā Devi by the palace established by King Shudrak. If you offer your son as sacrifice to this Chandikā, then the King will not die. Then he would live for another hundred years. If you do it tonight, only then it will be effective, otherwise not."

Birwar said to the earth, "O Devi! I'll now return home to perform the sacrifice tonight."

Prithvi said, "Be blessed my son!" and she vanished.

The King who followed Birwar heard every bit of it. The king further followed Birwar up to his house.

At home, Birwar woke up his wife, Dharmawati, and narrated the whole incident. Birwar woke up his son and broke the news about the need for instant sacrifice. He said, "O Son! The king will remain alive only if you are sacrificed to Goddess Chandikā, otherwise he would die on the third day." Though, he was still a child he proved his name Shakidhar meaningful. He said, "Father! I would be a blessed child if my life can save the king. It would also be a gesture of reciprocation to the King whose hands are feeding us. Why are you delaying things? Let us go at once and offer me as a gift to Bhagawati. With that the King would be free from the bad omen."

Birwar was satisfied with that answer. He said, "You are my real son." He saluted the son and went to the temple of Chandikā with his son, daughter and wife. The King followed them secretly.

At the temple, Birwar placed his son before the Goddess. The son bowed to Chandikā, worshipped and then prayed to her, "O Goddess! After my death, let the King rule freely for another hundred years."

Birwar prayed, "With the sacrifice of my son, may the King live long!" saying so he sacrificed his son to the Goddess Chandikā. At that moment an aerial sound thundered. "There is no better devotee than you! O Birwar! You had only one son; by sacrificing that true son, you have given life and kingdom to the king."

All these happened in front of the eyes of the King. His sister Birwati embraced her deceased brother and she too died. Then Dharmawati said to her husband, "O Lord! Now, the service to the king is over. My daughter too has died of unbearable pain. Now, what is the use of my life as a childless woman? I was foolish enough that I did not sacrifice my head for the king. Now, permit me to enter the sacrificial pious fire."

Birwar heard her out and replied, "True there is no joy in living without our children. Wait for sometime. I will collect firewood and make a pyre for you." Birwar made a pyre and Dharmawati entered the pyre with prayers, "O Devi! Bless me that this very person would be my husband in my next life too. And King Shudrak would be free from the bad omen." Praying so, she fell into the flames and embraced death.

Then, Birwar too prayed. After the prayers, Birwar took his sword and cut off his head in one powerful stroke.

King Shudrak was watching all these and fell in agony and bewilderment. He thought, "O! I have never seen such a ghastly sight or have heard anything like this. This sage has performed a disastrous deed by wiping out his family for the sake of my longevity. Who else in this world can show such sagacity and courage like him? If I fail to repay him, then what is the use of life and the kingdom? There is no benefit in living like an animal! Everyone will talk ill of me because I lost courage!"

Thinking like this, King Shudrak took out his sword and went up to the Goddess and prayed, "O Devi! I have always lived under your shelter; be pleased with the gift of this body and bless that Birwar, the greatest among the warriors, full of virtuous qualities who sacrificed himself and his family for me, to make him come to life." He said so and raised his sword to cut off his head when the aerial voice said, "Son! Don't try to do it! I'm pleased with the courage that you have shown! I bless that Birwar comes to life along with his wife, daughter and son." The moment the aerial sound ceased; each one came back to life with complete body. The King stood secretly out of sight. He was weeping but the tears were of pleasure that Birwar and his family had regained their lives. Secretly he looked at them again and again. It was very difficult for him to control his happiness.

Birwar was in illusion. He thought that it must have been a long sleep and a nightmare. He could not believe his eyes. He called them one by one by their name to make sure that they are alive, "How did you come alive after certain death? Is it my illusion or the blessing of the Goddess?" His wife and children confirmed that it was the blessing of the Goddess Chandikā that got them the life back; they are alive and talking. Birwar accepted it, "Yes, it must have happened only because of her mercy and blessings!"

They all bowed to the Goddess, worshipped and prayed and happily returned home. Birwar left them safe at home and returned to his duty. King Shudrak, having observed all, returned to his palace too. When he saw Birwar he asked, "Who is there at the Singhdwār?"

Birwar answered, "O Lord! It is I, Birwar. I obeyed your order and went to the weeping woman. She was one from the demons. She vanished when she saw and heard me."

The king was astonished to hear that. He had been a witness to each happening and yet the brave and courageous warrior was not willing to take credit for it. They are extraordinary persons who perform extraordinary deeds and yet never mention it.

The king was satisfied. He returned to the palace to spend the rest of the night. The next morning when Birwar came to the court to pay his routine visit, the king called the attention of all ministers and courtiers and narrated the events that took place during the night. All the courtiers called, Bravo in unison. 'He is a sage, certainly a sage.' After that, the king divided his kingdom in two equal parts and made Birwar the king of half his territory. Thereafter, they ruled well for a longtime.

Vetāla finished the story and asked, "O Emperor! Tell me, whose sacrifice is the best sacrifice! If you wouldn't answer knowingly, then the previous curse will take over."

The King answered the Vetāla, "Oh, that belongs to the world of Spirits! King Shudrak is the greatest among them."

"But why?" Vetāla asked again, "Why not Birwar who has no peer on the earth? Or why is his wife not the best? She had to see her son being killed like an animal and yet she did not lose heart. And why don't you take Shaktidhar, the son, to be the best that despite being a child he showed great courage? Then why do you claim Shudrak to be the best among them?"

The king said again, "Birwar belonged to a highly refined and cultured family. It was his pious duty to save his master with his life or those of his family members. His wife too belonged to an illustrious family and treated her husband greater than her own life. That is why she followed her husband and performed her duty. Shaktidhar was their son, and had the blood of that high family. The quality of the finished cloth depends on the quality of the thread. On the other hand, Kings usually save themselves by sacrificing their servants and employees. But here, Shudrak is offered to sacrifice his life for a servant and his family. Shudrak is the best among them."

Vetāla heard the King's reply intently and vanished from his shoulder, and retreated to the tree where he resided. Without getting bewildered by supernatural show of Vetāla, the King decided to take him to the Monk, that very night.

> *'Management Control basically means fi nance control, quality control, inventory control, control of production and human resource.'*

5

Executives grow from a seed, big as a tree,
In leaves and fruits they find subtle entry,
Their branches grow strong. They synthesize all:
Into a seed, and become complete and free.

The Marriage of Soma Prabhā

Vikram Sen reached that rosewood tree and picked up the human corpse with laughing Vetāla in it, put it up on his shoulder; and confidently and fearlessly, free from the feelings of carrying a dead body, walked towards the Buddha Monk.

The Vetāla on the shoulders of King Vikram said, "O Emperor! You are determined and handsome in appearance. I'm impressed by your devotion. So, I'm telling another story to keep off your tiredness from the tough journey in this dark night."

Ujjaini was a world famous city where a king named Punya Sen reigned. His favourite Minister was Hariswami, a Brahmin of great qualities. He had a virtuous wife; able son Deva Swami; and beautiful daughter Soma Prabhā of enchanting charm.

When his daughter reached puberty she acquired greater beauty and ego. Once, through her mother, she sent a message to her father and brother, "I should be given to a great warrior or a very learned person or to an expert scientist. I wouldn't survive if I am given to some inferior figure." Her father started the search but was not successful; instead he fed up. Once, the King sent the minister to make a deal with another king in a distant land. There he was approached by a young Brahmin man infatuated by the tales of the beauty of his daughter and asked for her hand in marriage. The father said, "My daughter will marry a great warrior or a very learned person or an expert scientist. What are you?"

The Brahmin young man said, "I know science."

The father said: "Then please show it."

On the request of the minister the young Brahmin created a chariot that could fly in the air; and he boarded that magical chariot with Hariswami; showed him heavenly places and returned. Hariswami accepted his proposal and promised to give his daughter in marriage. He fixed a date for the coming week.

On the same day, in Ujjaini, an youth asked Devaswami to give his sister in marriage to him. Devaswami said, "My sister will marry a great warrior or a very learned person or an expert scientist. What are you?" The youth claimed he was a warrior. He showed him the art of weaponry and impressed him. Devaswami accepted his proposal and promised to give his sister in marriage. He fixed a date for the next week and invited him.

On the same day, another Brahmin youth turned up and asked for the hand of her daughter. The mother said, "My daughter will marry a great warrior or a very learned person or an expert scientist. What are you?" "I'm a learned man," the Brahmin youth claimed, and the mother accepted him and invited him to come after a week.

Next day, when Hariswami returned home, who informed all that he had met a young scientist and given his word to marry off Soma Prabhā, they also informed him that they too selected a young warrior and a young scholar to marry Soma Prabhā. Apparently, Hariswami was in a dilemma how three grooms can marry one girl.

On the seventh day, all the three youth came to the house of Hariswami. But something strange had occurred there. Soma Prabhā was missing. Everyone was worried. Immediately, the learned youth started calculating and announced, "She has been kidnapped by a Demon named Dhumrashikha and has kept her at his abode in the forest of Vindhyāchal Mountain Range. Hariswami was worried and in great fear. He asked the scientist for a way out. He created a warrior's chariot filled up with different weapons and sent Hariswami, the warrior and the scholar to the forest of the Vinghya. The learned man easily searched out the abode of the demon Dhumrashikha. The demon was angry to see them at his abode. He roared and attacked them. The warrior and Hariswami fought a pitched battle with the demon. Though, the demon had great strength, he was an extraordinary fighter. The warrior cut off his head and took Soma Prabhā and returned.

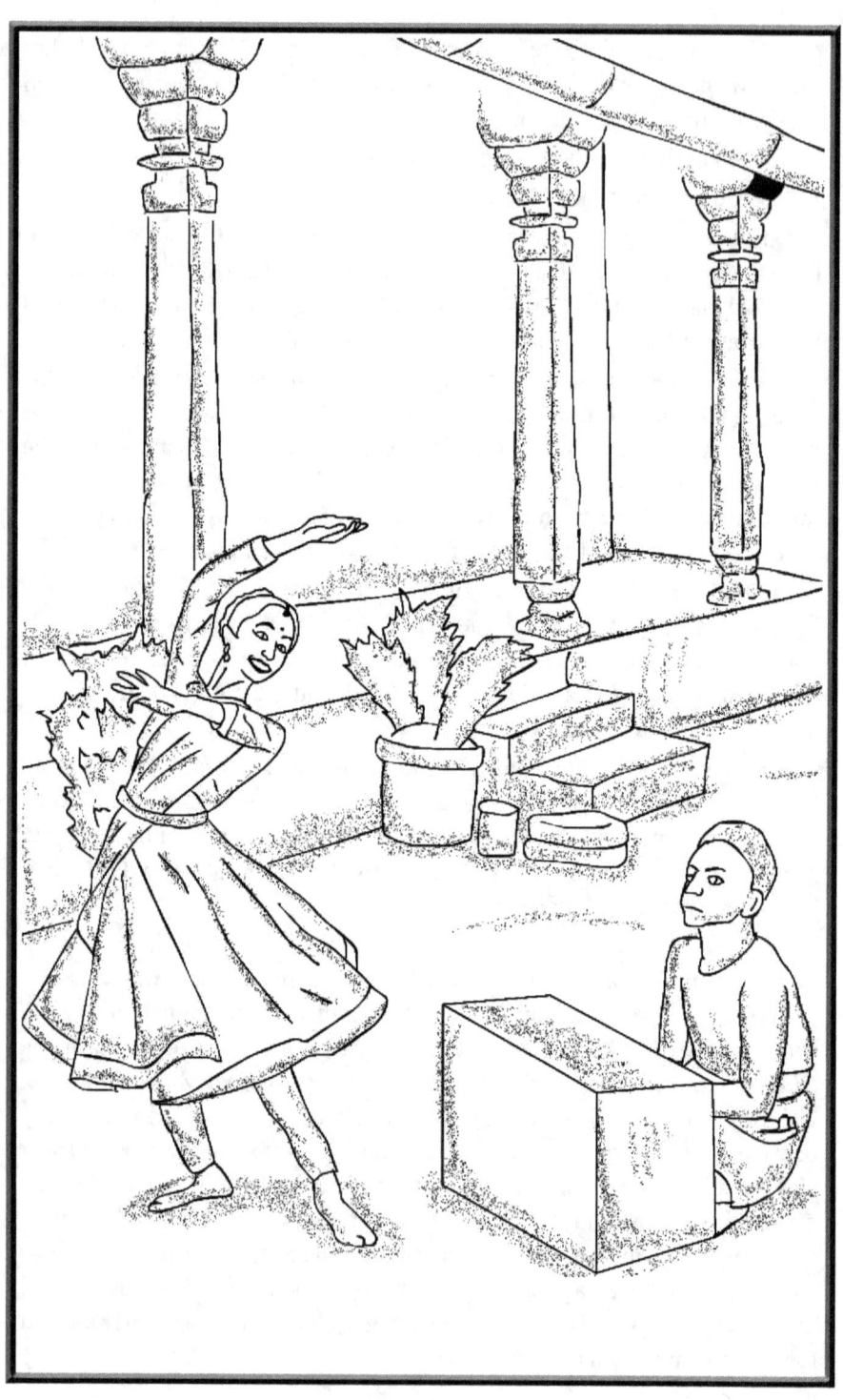

At the time of marriage, a serious debate started, "Who would marry Soma Prabhā?"

The learned man claimed, "Had I not calculated the whereabouts of Soma Prabhā, others wouldn't have been able to bring her back from such a secret place. So, she should be given to me."

The scientist claimed, "Had I not created the chariot able to fly in air, then none would have been able to reach there within no time like the gods. Without a chariot, the chariot fight was not possible. Because of only that Soma Prabhā has been brought back. So, she should be given to me."

The warrior claimed, "Had I not killed that demon in the battle, who else would have been successful in bringing her to this place. I have greater claim. She should be given to me only."

Hariswami was bewildered at the turn of events and the conflicting claims. He was unable to decide on the right person for his daughter.

Having finished the story Vetāla asked, "O Emperor! Tell me, whom should Soma Prabhā be given in marriage? If you knowingly evade the answer, then your head will splinter into hundred pieces."

Vikram heard Vetāla and answered him "The warrior should be given the girl in marriage. He endangered his life and with his physical power conquered the demon and freed the girl. The scholar and the scientists were appointed to help the girl and the warrior. They cannot make any personal claim. You see, the astrologers (like the learned man) and carpenters (like the scientist) work for others. They are only instrumental in achieving something. Is it not?"

Vetāla heard it and vanished from his shoulder, and went to the tree where he resided. Without getting bewildered from the supernatural and magical show of Vetāla, the king decided to take him to the Monk, that very night.

matters most.

> *'Budgets are expressions of desires for accomplishing something defi nite; and wish to work on a designed pattern.'*

6

The employees are for result, not for fun,
Should be straight as the barrel of a new gun,
They must calculate and never speculate:
And successfully, in time, get the work done.

Dhawal and Madan Sundari

Slowly but surely king Vikram Sen reached that rosewood tree and picked up the human corpse with laughing Vetāla on it; put it up on his shoulder; walked briskly but silently towards the Buddha Monk.

The Vetāla on the shoulders of King Vikram said, "O Emperor! You have fallen in some unnatural pain. Yet I'm pleased with you and impressed by your devotion and constant effort. For this very reason, I'm telling another story for your entertainment."

During the ancient times, there was a king on the earth named Yashah Ketu. In the capital Shobhāwati there was a very beautiful Gauri temple. On its southern flank was a big pond named Gauri Teertha.

Every year on the 14th day of Moonlit (Shukla Paksha) of Āshādha gentle, humble, rich and religious persons from all the four directions used to come there to take holy dip in that famous and pious pond, Gauri Teertha.

Once, a washer man called Dhawal, who was the son of Vimal, from village Brahmasthal came to take holy bath in Gauri Teertha pond. He saw Madan Sundari, the daughter of Shuddhapatta, a washer man. She was more beautiful than the moon as she was a living symbol of Cupid.

Madan Sundari stole his heart and he was affected by intense passion. He enquired about the girl, collected all information and returned to his parents. His parents found him not keeping good health.

Dhawal conveyed his wish to his mother and father. The father came to him and announced that, "O my son! It's not a problem. I know her father Shuddhapatta. He also knows me. He won't refuse if I go there and ask for the hand of his daughter in marriage. It's not a tough work."

In this way he consoled his son and forced him to take his meal. One day, along with his son he visited the place of Shuddhapatta and asked for the hand of his daughter for Dhawal. With all grace and honour he accepted the genuine proposal.

On an auspicious day, Shuddhapatta gave his daughter, an equal match, to Dhawal. He brought her to his parents' house, and lived a very happy and satisfied life.

One day, the brother of Madan Sundari came to meet them and invite them home as they were planning to perform a *yagya*. The brother-in-law stayed there for the night.

The next morning Dhawal started for the house of his in-laws along with his wife and brother-in law. They reached the city of Shobhāwati and saw the great temple of Gauri. He asked them to wait for him. He would go inside and perform worship of the deity. All of them were ready to pray to the Goddess. But Dhawal was the first to go inside. They waited for him.

Dhawal went inside to worship the Goddess. When he stood before the large idol of the Goddess with eighteen hands and a weapon in each hand he remembered how she brought Mahishāsur under her feet and smashed him to death. His body quivered at some celestial sensation. He got some spiritual inspiration. His conscience said, "People sacrifice different living beings to please the Goddess; why should not I sacrifice myself in order to please her. The idea flashed in him. He went inside an empty room, brought out a sharp and bright sword and cut his own head off on the feet of the Goddess.

It was definitely a long wait for the brother and sister outside the temple. "Why is he late?" They enquired each other and the brother went inside for knowing the reason for delay. He was shocked and felt intense pain after seeing beheaded body of his sister's husband. He was unsure what he will say to his young sister who has become widow. Out of severe passion he too picked up the sword and cut off his own head.

When the brother too did not return, Madan Sundari decided to go inside the temple to find out the reason. She saw the heads and bodies of her husband and brother lying unattended at separate places. "Oh Goddess!

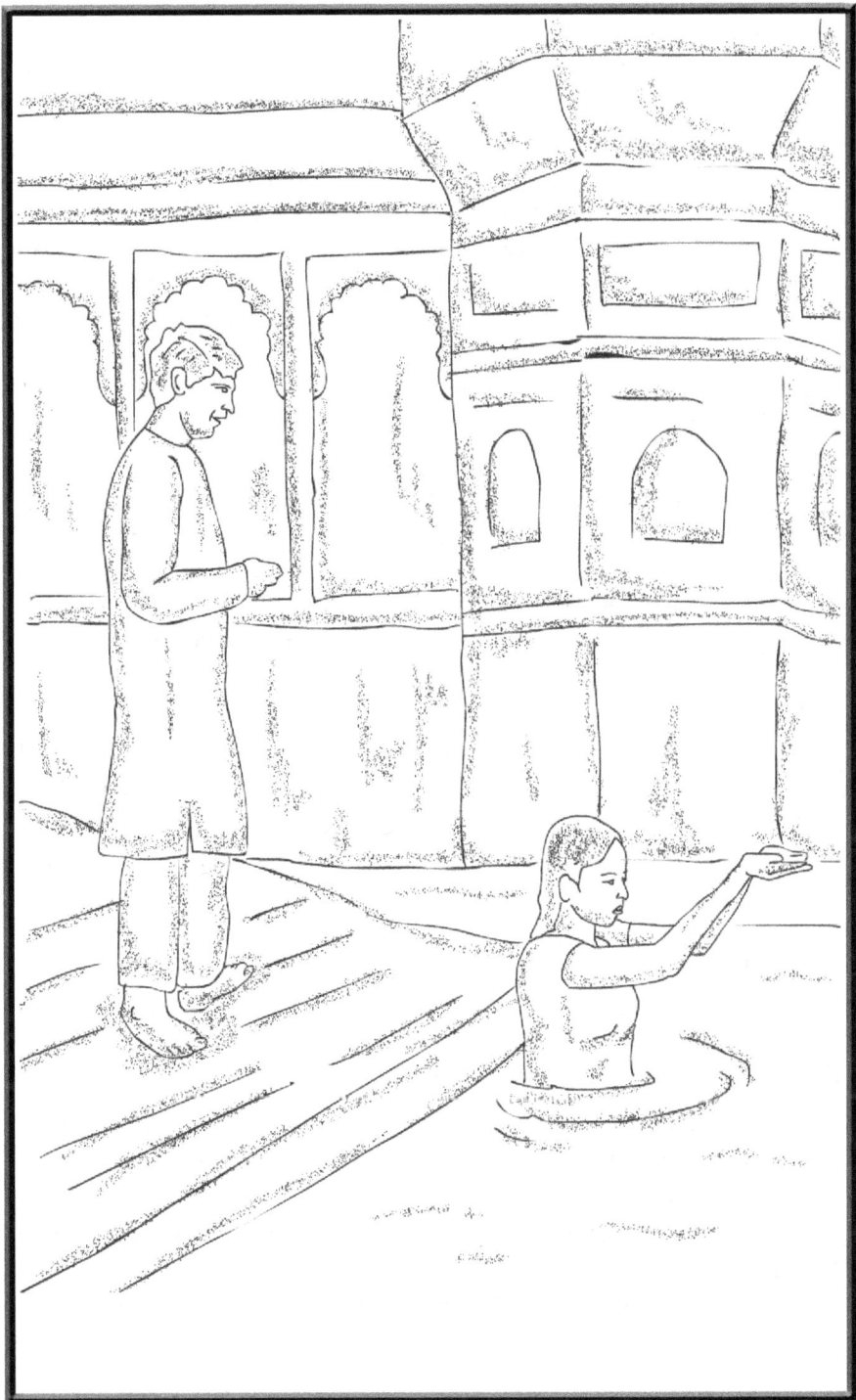

What has happened?" She fell flat at the feet of the Goddess and started weeping bitterly. She could not think clearly. It came to her mind, "Now, what is the use of my life when I have lost both my husband and brother?"

She was now mentally ready to leave her body. She started praying to the Goddess, "O Devi! You are the deity to give life, character and household! You are the Goddess that keeps one married for a long time! You are the half of the body of Lord Shiva! You are the shelter of all women! You take off the pain! Why then suddenly you killed both my husband and brother? It was not good of you! I have incessantly worshipped you! I am your devotee! O Listen to me! You gave shelter to me! I have some simple things to say! I am leaving behind this body here at your feet! Wherever I take new birth, these should be my husband and brother as they are now!"

She prayed like that; bowed to the Goddess; went out and prepared the knot for hanging herself to a tree of Ashoka. When she was about to insert her head into the knot, there came an aerial voice, "O Daughter! Don't show such courage! You're a child and yet have shown the courage to sacrifice yourself! This excessive courage has pleased me! Leave this knot there; and join the heads of your husband and brother with their respective bodies. I bless them, they will become alive!"

Madan Sundari started weeping out of pleasure. She hurried back to the idol and hurriedly joined the heads and bodies. In such impatience and hurry by mistake she joined the head of her husband to the body of her brother and the head of her brother to the body of her husband.

They came alive and were ecstatic in joy. They prostrated before the Goddess and went out with Madan Sundari. It was then she realized what mistake had she committed by joining wrong head to wrong body. She was again at her wit's end.

Vetāla paused for a second and then asked, "Tell me now, which body should be the husband of that lady? If you knowingly avoid the answer the curse given earlier will come true."

Vikram answered, "Among all our organs the head is the most important, so, the body in which his head is joined will be her husband as only the head can recognize who is what?"

Vetāla heard it and vanished from his shoulder, and went to the tree where he resided. Without getting bewildered from the supernatural and magical show of Vetāla, the king decided to take him to the Monk, that very night.

management process.

> 'Coordination is the synchronization of the efforts of organs to provide timely execution of the common purpose of an organization.'

7

An entrepreneur must be trained to train,
And possess latent power to maintain,
He should change the course to best advantage
And should be only energy, ability and brain

King Chanda Singh and the Royal Servant

Slowly and surely King Vikram Sen reached that rosewood tree and picked up the human corpse inhabited by Vetāla; put it on his shoulder and walked silently but fearlessly towards the Buddha Monk again.

The Vetāla said, "O Emperor! You don't realise what you are doing. Yet I'm pleased with you and impressed by your devotion and constant effort. For this very reason, I'm telling you another story to keep you engaged."

On the eastern seashore was a famous city called Tāmralipti where a ruler named Chanda Singh reigned. He was a valiant warrior; ethical and aloof from the women of others. He was ruthless with enemies but never destroyed crops or personal wealth of any person.

Once, a Kshatriya named Satwasheel came to meet the King. He was in rags and said, "I am your servant but extremely poor." Despite the pitiable condition, he neither demanded hike in wages nor any gifts. His thoughts were, "Why I'm in such penury despite my birth in a royal family. Though poor why did the Creator instill me with such high ambitions."

After a few months, the King went on a hunting expedition, followed by an army of horsemen and infantry. At the forest, the King chased a big wild pig and strayed away from his team of security and soldiers. The path in the forest was grassy and rugged. Having lost his way back, the King disembarked from the horse and sat under a tree.

Meanwhile, the Kshatriya servant in rags was following the King on foot ignoring his own safety. Finally he saw the King. The King asked him, "Well gentleman, you are following me like this, how do you know the path?"

The man said with folded hands, "O King! Yes, I know the way but please take some rest. Suryadeva is shining hot and bright as the middle jewel in the sky-bride's necklace."

The King agreed and asked him to fetch some water to drink. The man in rags affirmed, climbed up a tall tree and spotted a river. The King preferred to take a bath and asked him to feed the horse. When the King finished his bath, Satwasheel came forward with two pieces of *āmlā* (myrobalan-a medicinal fruit); rinsed them and humbly requested him to eat them.

"O Satwasheel! You are really the essence of morality as your name suggests. What more can I say?"

The King felt sympathy for the man in rags and reluctantly accepted the fruits. He ate them; drank water; took rest for some time and started his journey back to the capital city.

In the court, the King honoured that man in rags; gave him lot of wealth. Still the King felt indebted to him for those two *āmlā* fruits. The King made him the personal bodyguard and Satwasheel soon shed the rags and became the close, royal confidante of the King.

Time passed. In the meantime, King decided to propose to the Princess of Singhal and sent Satwasheel as his emissary. Satwasheel boarded the ship bound for Singhal. The journey went smooth until it reached the deep sea where a huge elephant in gold, carrying multiple flags was floating on the sea water. Immediately, clouds began to engulf the area and it was raining cats and dogs. High velocity winds lashed; the ship was in danger; the panicked crew anchored the ship to the pillars of the flags on the elephant.

The sea was becoming more turbulent; high tides increased and the elephant started diving into the sea and the ship started sinking. Amidst the chaos, Satwasheel decided to act; he identified the place where the elephant dived and jumped into the roaring sea with a naked sword in hand.

The roaring wind and heavy currents had already thrown the ship astride; the ship got smashed into pieces. Tragedy had struck; most passengers on board fell prey to the fury of the wild sea-creatures even as Satwasheel was diving deeper and deeper.

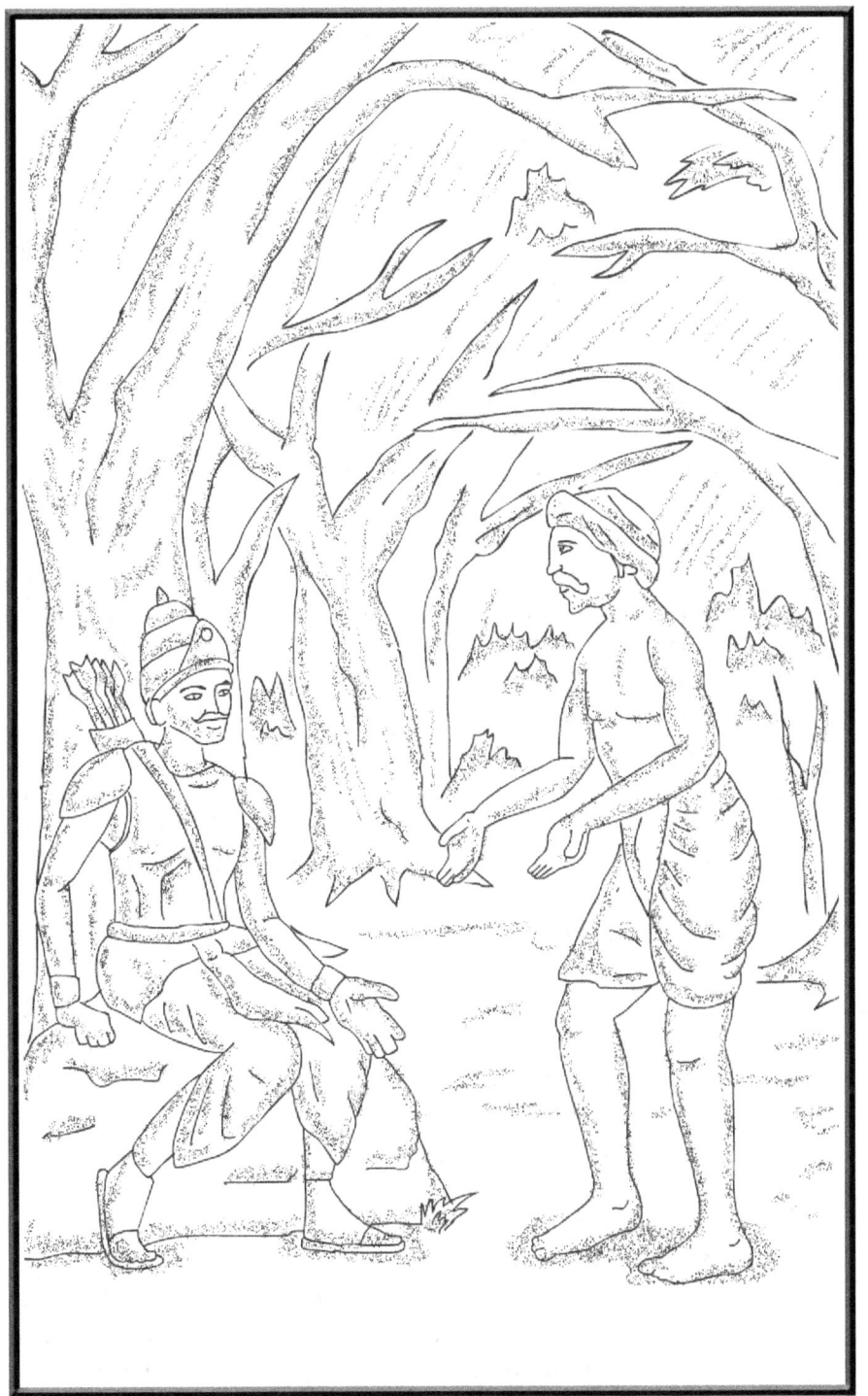

Deep down, what Satwasheel saw was amazing – a beautiful city: glowing brightly with jewelled pillars; nice and attractive buildings made of gold; clean ponds with stairs finished in rare stones; colourful gardens adding glitter to the city; walls sparkling with jewels, pictures and bright flags.

Satwasheel spotted a large temple of Goddess Durgā on a Sumeru-like mountain and entered it and bowed to the Goddess. After worshipping the deity he sat there thinking, "What a magical marvel has come before my eyes!"

At that moment, a beautiful girl, with lotus eyes, moon-like face, flower-like smile, and tender like lotus plant, entered the temple followed by thousands of girls. She worshipped the deity and left the temple; but her beauty touched the heart of Satwasheel. He followed her to another attractive building of luxury. He found her sitting inside on a jewelled bed; he went closer to her and sat like a statue looking at her enchanting face.

One of her maids saw his actions and understood his passion for the princess. She asked, "O Gentleman! You have reached here, so you are our respectable guest. Now enjoy the hospitality offered by our mistress. Please get up, take bath and have food." Unsuspectingly he went to the pond and dived into the pond, and Lo! he came out of the pond of Tāmralipti, the kingdom of Chanda Singh.

Satwasheel wondered, "How was he transported to that place? What has happened? Where is that beautiful garden? Where is that nectar-like encounter with the dame? Why have I been given a poison of separation from my sweetheart? Is it a dream? Am I waking or sleeping? No, no, that maid has cheated me. I'm in illusion." He wandered in the garden crying for the princess, like a mad man.

A palace guard informed the King, Chanda Singh. When the King came, he found his bodyguard in a nervous state. He consoled him and asked, "O friend! What happened? Where were you going? How have you come here? Where have you been? Where have you fallen?"

Satwasheel narrated the complete incident. The King thought that this man had been badly punished by Cupid. The King took it as the best opportunity to repay his debt. The King declared, "O Friend! Don't worry! I will take you to that princess through that very route."

Next day, the King and Satwasheel boarded a ship and reached the deep sea. In the middle of the deep sea the big golden elephant with flags came closer. Satwasheel said, "O King! This is the big elephant with wonderful magical power. I will dive first and you should follow me." Saying so, Satwasheel dived first; the King followed.

They reached the wonder city and saw the wonderful sights. They entered the great temple where the King performed *poojā* and sat with Satwasheel waiting for the princess. After a while, the Princess was seen entering the temple as a living incarnation of light surrounded by her friends.

Satwasheel exclaimed, "She is the beauty!" The King understood his craze for that beauty. The Princess also saw that man and thought: 'Who can he be, the man with divine and sublime qualities and body? He must be someone very special with rare attributes.' She entered the temple to complete the ritual. But the King ignored the Princess and came out into the garden.

The Princess performed her *poojā* and requested the deity to give her a suitable husband, and came out. She called one of her friends and said, "O Dear! Where is he? I saw him here. Where has that sage gone? Please request him to accept our hospitality. He looks very honourable."

When the request was communicated, the King ignored her and said in ironical tone, "O Humble lady! You have completed all your hospitality with words. We don't need anything more."

The friend returned to the Princess, and conveyed the message. The Princess wondered how come the King was completely detached to the rare hospitality that is unthinkable for a human being. She felt deeply attracted towards the King but she showed patience. She remembered her prayer to Goddess Pārvati for a suitable husband and thought it to be an opportune moment. To persuade the King, she herself entered the garden and prayed to the King to accept the hospitality.

The King, knowing what happened to Satwasheel said, "O Humble Girl! This man informed me about the Goddess here. I had to visit that temple and worship the Goddess. We followed the lead of wonderful flags on magical golden elephant and came to pray to Goddess Gauri. Later on we saw you too."

In response the Princess said, "O King! Then only for the sake of adventure please come and see the most wonderful city in the three worlds."

The king laughed to hear it and said, "He had informed about the city too. It has a beautiful pond for bathing."

The Girl said, "O King! Don't think like that. I wouldn't deceive you. Honourable persons will never be deceived. I am attracted by your great courage. Please, do not refuse my request." The King accepted the invitation and went to the glowing cave. It was yet another beautiful city in the valley of a Sumeru-like mountain that had flowers blooming for all seasons; built up with rare stones and jewels. The King was requested to sit on a jewel-bedecked throne. The King got a royal welcome in the traditional way with lamps, etc. When the formalities were completed, the Princess said, "O Great men! I'm the daughter of the demon king Kālanemi. Lord Vishnu killed him and sent him to heaven. These twin cities were built by none other than Lord Viswakarmā himself. The town fulfills all desires."

The Princess dedicated all her wealth to the King, who in turn told the Princess, "If it is so, then you are my daughter. I will give you in marriage to this great warrior friend of mine Satwasheel." She bowed to her new father and accepted the blessings. She humbly replied, "I'll obey you."

The King solemnised the marriage of the Princess and Satwasheel. The happy King said to Satwasheel: "O Friend! I have paid the debt of one *āmlā* that you gave me. I will still be grateful to you for the other fruit." Satwasheel bowed to the king.

Then, the king said to the Princess, "O Good Girl! Now, show me my way so that I can reach my kingdom safely. The Princess gifted a sword called 'indomitable' and a fruit that keeps one free from old age and death. The king gladly accepted them and dived into the magical pond, and reached his kingdom safely. Satwasheel ruled the twin cities with his wife, the Princess.

After finishing the story, Vetāla asked King Vikram, "O Emperor! In the respect of diving into the unknown deep sea who between the two had greater courage: the King or Satwasheel".

Vikram heard it intently with due attention. He answered; "Out of the two, in my opinion, Satwasheel has greater courage than the King. When he dived into the sea, he knew nothing about the city but when the King dived he knew everything in advance and was not afraid of the consequences."

The King had disobeyed Vetāl's diktat as he had broken the silence. So, Vetāla heard it and vanished from his shoulder and went back to the tree again. Without showing any unease from the supernatural and magical show of Vetāla, the King decided to take him to the Monk, that very night. Dedicated men of patience never worry about obstacles; they keep trying hard for the completion of their task.

chance of depending on chance.

In management, tried and tested methods are preferred. The

and is in great demand because of the proportion of business that

and the job to be taken on the other. It is the inner and deeper

entrepreneurship.

'Selection is the process to identify persons with a greater likelihood of success in the job to be given.'

8

Executives get not swept by wind nor burns by blaze,
An executive makes immediate present a joyous phase,
Enjoys working in troubles, hardships, emergencies
And works steadily and laughs on and off the work-stage.

The Sons of Vishnuswāmi

King Vikram Sen reached the rosewood tree again and picked up the human corpse with laughing Vetāla in it, put it up on the shoulder and walked confidently and fearlessly. The King was silent as he wanted to complete the task assigned by the Buddha Monk. The Vetāla lying on the dead body said, "O Emperor! You don't know what you are doing. Still I am pleased with your devotion and consistent effort. For this very reason, I'm telling another story to keep you refreshed."

There was a country called Brikkaghata where a very rich Brahmin, Vishnuswāmi, lived with three sons from his noble wife. When the sons grew young and became of marriageable age, the Brahmin performed a *yagya*.

As a result of the *yagya*, he sent a tortoise and asked his three sons to catch it and bring it back to the place of *yagya* for its completion. Otherwise, the *yagya* may lose its effect.

The three brothers went to the designated place and searched out the tortoise. The eldest brother, addressing the younger brothers said, "One of you should catch the tortoise and take it to the place of *yagya*. I cannot catch it as I cannot stand its smell as raw meat."

The brothers too refused, saying, "O Brother! If you hate it, then why should we?" The elder brother said again, "You two catch the tortoise;

otherwise you will be responsible for destroying the *yagya* of father and go to hell with him."

The younger brothers laughed at him, "O Brother! You know our duties well, but have forgotten your own duty."

The elder brother gazed at their ignorance, "What? Don't you know my tastes about food? I'm very sophisticated in food. How can I touch this hateful creature?"

Having heard it, the second brother said, "I am very sensitive. How can I touch it?" When the second brother refused then the elder brother turned towards the youngest one, "You are younger to both of us. Pick up this tortoise."

The youngest brother raised his eyebrows in anger, "O Fools! I'm most delicate about my stuffed bed." The three sons were tender and had delicate sensitivities in their respective fields.

They had their ego too. So, they fought and eluded a consensus. For a final decision they went straight to Vitankpur, which was the capital of king Prasenajeet and narrated the complete incident. The king pronounced, "Stay in my palace. First I'll test you three?"

They said in unison, "Okay, We will abide by it."

The King invited them for meals and ushered them into proper seats. They were served sixteen types of tasteful food with six types of aesthetic and chemical juices. When they were about to eat the food, the elder one twisted his mouth and nose in disgust and refused to eat. The King asked, "Why don't you eat such delicious food."

On being asked by the King, he exclaimed that the meal has the smell of burnt dead body; and he would not eat it. He said, "O King! The rice has the foul smell of burnt dead body. So, despite the fact that it is delicious, I do not like to eat it."

Others too smelt it but declared it fragrant and known by the name *kamal*. An enquiry by the King revealed that the paddy was from a field closer to a burning *ghāta* or crematorium. He was amazed at the declaration of the elder brother who defied the fragrance of the rice and traced its origin. The King announced, "O Brahmin! You are really very sophisticated about your food. You are being given some other food. Take it."

It was clear that the eldest brother had very powerful sensitivity for smell. After the meals they were sent to take rest. A high profile prostitute was sent to the room of the second brother who had extreme sensitivities on

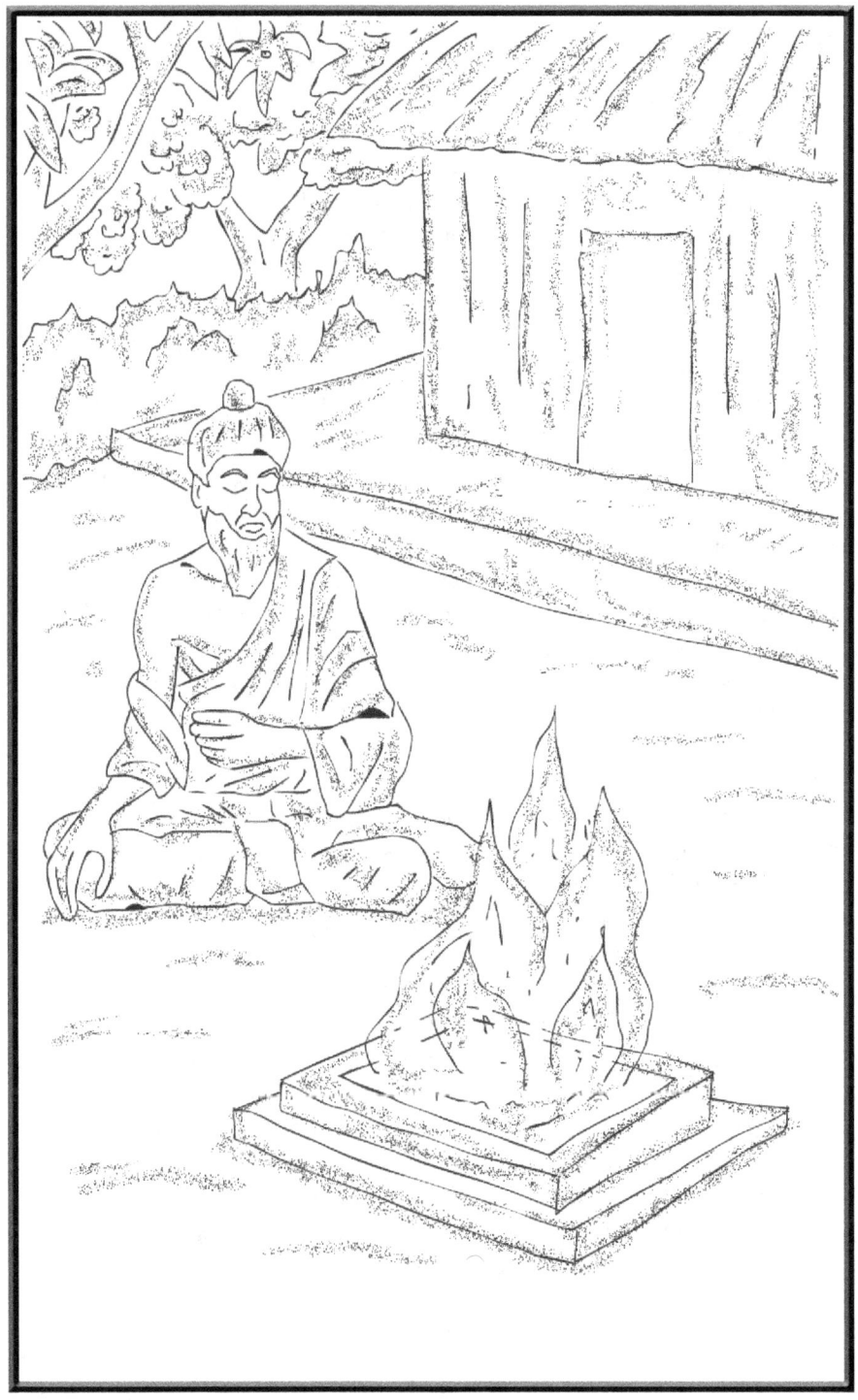

women. She was well dressed; had nice makeup; wore attractive ornaments and exuded fragrance. She entered the illuminated bedroom of the brother on orders from the king.

As soon as the brother smelt the fragrance emanating from the woman he closed his nose with fingers and expressed signs of extreme discomfort. He directed the servants to shoo her away as she had the foul smell of goats; if she is not thrown out, he would faint. His fiery and pungent sense perceived what was not apparent to others.

The courtiers brought her to the King and narrated the whole episode to the King. The King called that brother and checked the facts; the lady confessed that as a child she had lost her mother and was raised on goat's milk. The King was awe-struck at the revelation. He praised the fine sensibility of the man and his sharp sense of smell.

The third one was treated royally. A special bed with seven soft mattresses; freshly washed white smooth sheet and soft pillows were provided to the youngest brother. He slept well on the bed but woke up in the middle of night, holding something in his left side and cried in pain. It was a reddish patch as an imprint of folded hair. The King was duly informed who ordered strict checking of the mattresses to find out something amiss. And, Lo! On the seventh mattress there was a hair folded in the same manner as seen on the youngest brother's body. They showed it to the King. Next morning the King announced that these Brahmins had wonderful senses and sensibilities. He announced an award of one lakh gold coin each."

The brothers got the wealth and their needs fulfilled. However, they forgot about the tortoise for their father's *yagya*. They became sinners but spent their life happily.

Vetāla told this wonderful story and enquired, "O Emperor! Remember the curse pronounced earlier, then give me the answer, who among the three brothers, has more keen and subtle and delicate sense?" Vikram heard every bit of it, intently with extra concentration. He answered immediately, "I feel that the youngest brother possessed an evolved sense than the others because it was he who felt the imprint of the folded hair as an impression on his body. As far as others are concerned, they had knowledge of the sources. There are chances that they knew it before also."

Vetāla heard the reply and disappeared from his shoulder, and went back the tree he resided. Without any bewilderment at the supernatural show of Vetāla, the King decided to take him to the Monk, that very night.

The *yagya*

from inside.

'*Organizational development is a change of attitude and structure to adapt to new technology, staff, market and challenges.*'

9

Each leaf of every branch is a part of him,
Lighted quite well or in shade almost dim,
Not as a part, the executives live as a whole:
The firm's ray they are, and they reflect the beam.

King Veeradeva

King Vikram Sen reached that rosewood tree and picked up the human corpse on which the Vetāla resides and walked fearlessly towards the Buddha Monk.

The Vetāla said to the King, "I am pleased with your devotion and constant effort. For that very reason, I'm telling another story to keep you refreshed."

In the region of Avanti, there was a city named Padmāwati during Satyayuga; it was called Bhogawati during Tretāyuga and Hiranyawati during Dwāpar yuga. In the Kaliyug it is called Ujjaini. A king name Veeradeva ruled over it. His queen was Padmarati.

One day, the King and the queen went into a penance at the banks of the sacred river Ganges with a wish to get a son. Their penance continued for many years. One day they heard a soliloquy, "O King! You will be blessed with a warrior son who will bear the family tradition; and you will also get a very beautiful daughter attractive than the nymphs."

Having heard this soliloquy, the King felt happy about the end result of his hard penance and returned to the capital city. In due course, his wife Padmarati delivered a son Shuradeva and in a few years came daughter Anagrati. True to the prediction, the daughter was so beautiful that even Kamadeva may find it difficult to escape her charms.

Both the children crossed adolescence; the King got serious about the marriage of his children as they grew young. He contacted all well to do Kings but none suited his daughter Anagrati. He sweetly said to his daughter, "O Putri! I have tried my best. Still I am not able to find a suitable groom for you. I think a *swayamvar* can help in selecting the right groom."

The daughter politely disagreed and announced, "O Father! I think *swayamvar* is something shameful. I don't like it. You can give my hand to any handsome man who knows science. But I am not interested in a person not having knowledge of any science or someone knowing many sciences."

Accordingly, the King started the search for a groom who met these stipulations. The news spread far and wide and it reached the southern province also. From there four handsome youth, who knew one science each came to the king. The King welcomed them and accorded great hospitality. The King asked them in the crowded court, "Please tell us one by one what science you know?"

The first one said, "I'm a Shudra. My name is Panchphuttika. All alone I can weave five pairs of fine cloth every day. I offer one to the God, one to a Brahmin, I keep one for myself, and one for the girl that will become my wife and I sell out the fifth one for a decent living. So, I claim that your daughter Anagwati should be given to me."

The second one said, "I'm a Vaishya. My name is Bhāshāsh. I understand and know the language of deer and all birds. So this Princess should be given to me."

Then, the third one said, "I'm Khangdhar, a Kshatriya. I have power and faith in my strong arms. There is hardly any warrior on this land who can compete with me in the battle of swords. So, your daughter should be given to me."

And then, the fourth one claimed, "O King! I'm a Brahmin named Jeevadatta. I restore life to any dead person in a few minutes. I am adept in this science. So, your daughter should accept me as her husband."

The King looked at all the handsome youth with interest but his mind was confused and whirled in the dilemma as to whom he should choose for the most beautiful daughter Anangrati.

Vetāla finished the story and asked the king, "O Emperor! Keep the curse pronounced earlier and then tell who among the four should be chosen as the husband of the Princess."

Vikram answered, "A Kshatriya girl should not be given to a Shudra. And how can she be given to the Vaishya who knows the language of deer

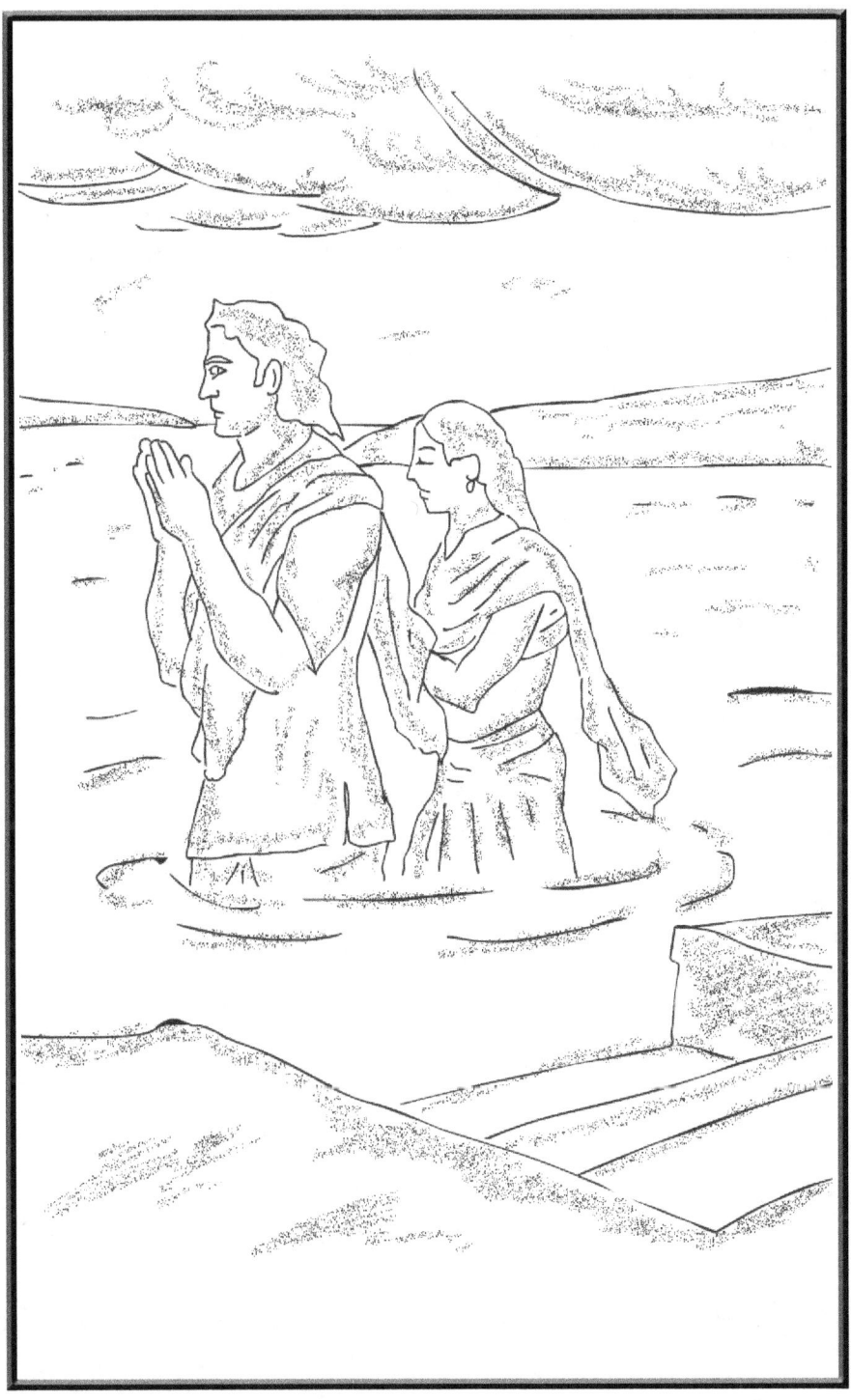

and birds. What is the use of that science? What is the value of the Brahmin who has fallen very low to become a magician? How can he be a powerful person? So, only a warrior can give security to the Princess, she can be given in marriage to him only."

Vetāla heard it and vanished from his shoulder, and returned to the tree where he resided. Without getting bewildered from the supernatural and magical show of Vetāla, the King was ready to take him to the Monk, that very night.

is behind bad decision making or indecisions on the part of an

'Only an energetic and confi dent mind is creative, and shows mastery; comes out with appropriate and apt solutions.'

10

An executive can't be impassioned or free from passion,
He definitely has one leg on crucifixion and one on adulation,
He must remain firm, un-swayed by success and failure
As there is a moment's difference in worship or vituperation.

Arthadatta, the Son of a Business Tycoon

Slowly and surely King Vikram Sen reached that rosewood tree, put the human corpse on the shoulder and walked silently but fearlessly towards the Buddha Monk in that dark night.

The Vetāla in the dead body said, "O Emperor! You are tired, so I am telling another story that will take off the fatigue and make you fresh.

There was a famous King named Veerbāhu, who was respected by all the kings. He was like Lord Indra, who rules Heaven. Veerbāhu had a grand capital city called Anangpur where a business tycoon named Arthadatta lived. His elder son was Dhandatta and his younger daughter was Madansenā.

One day Dharmadatta, the son of another business magnate got an opportunity to have a glimpse of Madansena's beauty. Her well shaped, hard pitchers-like breasts oozing seductive beauty intoxicated Dharmadatta. He felt bitten by the arrows of Cupid. Madansenā was walking on the roof of her palace. The day passed. But he remained engrossed in her beauty and her thoughts encircled his mind.

Dharmadatta returned engrossed in her thoughts and fell on the bed as if bitten by the moon rays. His friends and relatives tried to know the cause of his moroseness and pain but he refused to open up. In the morning he was again at the place of Madansenā and found her waiting for her friends in the garden. He went straight to her; fell at her feet and in sweet words he requested to get her love.

Madansenā was astonished but she maintained her calm. She said, "I'm a virgin; and for you I'm another person's betrothed wife as my father had promised to give me to Samudradatta (as deep and calm as sea), a businessman. Within a short time I will get married to him. So, silently go away so that none can see you otherwise, it will ruin me."

Having been rejected by her, Dharmadatta said in pain, "O Beauty! Whatever the position may be but I wouldn't live without you." She heard it but was afraid of losing her sanctity and virginity. But she added, "Then let my marriage be solemnised and let my father get the bliss of giving his virgin daughter in marriage, I'll come to you lovingly."

Dharmadatta heard it and could not decipher the meaning of it. He said, "I don't want a beloved enjoyed by others. The lotus may be clean but there is no pleasure in eating tasted food." She saw no way out so she promised, "Then I'll come to you just after marriage and only then I will go to my husband's chamber."

Dharmadatta asked her to commit that under an oath to be reassured. Bound in a deed of word, Dharmadatta left her and returned home. She too felt relieved and returned to her room.

Madansena's marriage was solemnized; she went to her husband's bed and lay there. But she did not embrace her husband Samudradatta who was lying nearby. When he requested her to show affection she started weeping and said, "O My Master! You are more beloved to me than my own life but listen to my request. Once I was alone in the garden when Dharmadatta, a friend of my brother stopped me and tried to propose. I saved myself from the temptations on the basis of the promise of my father that he will give a virgin daughter in marriage. But I promised to go to him after the marriage and then to the husband. Then, O my husband! Give me the order to go to him. I have to return soon. I have followed the path of truth since my childhood, I would not be able to break it when I'm mature."

Samudradatta was taken aback hearing her weird promise. He thought for a moment about his wife who was wedded to truth, "Fie! Fie! Fie upon her and me! She has her promise to keep. She has dared to say it to me. She is courageous enough to defy me and go to meet her lover at any cost. Then why should I break away from my own path of truth? Let her go. Why

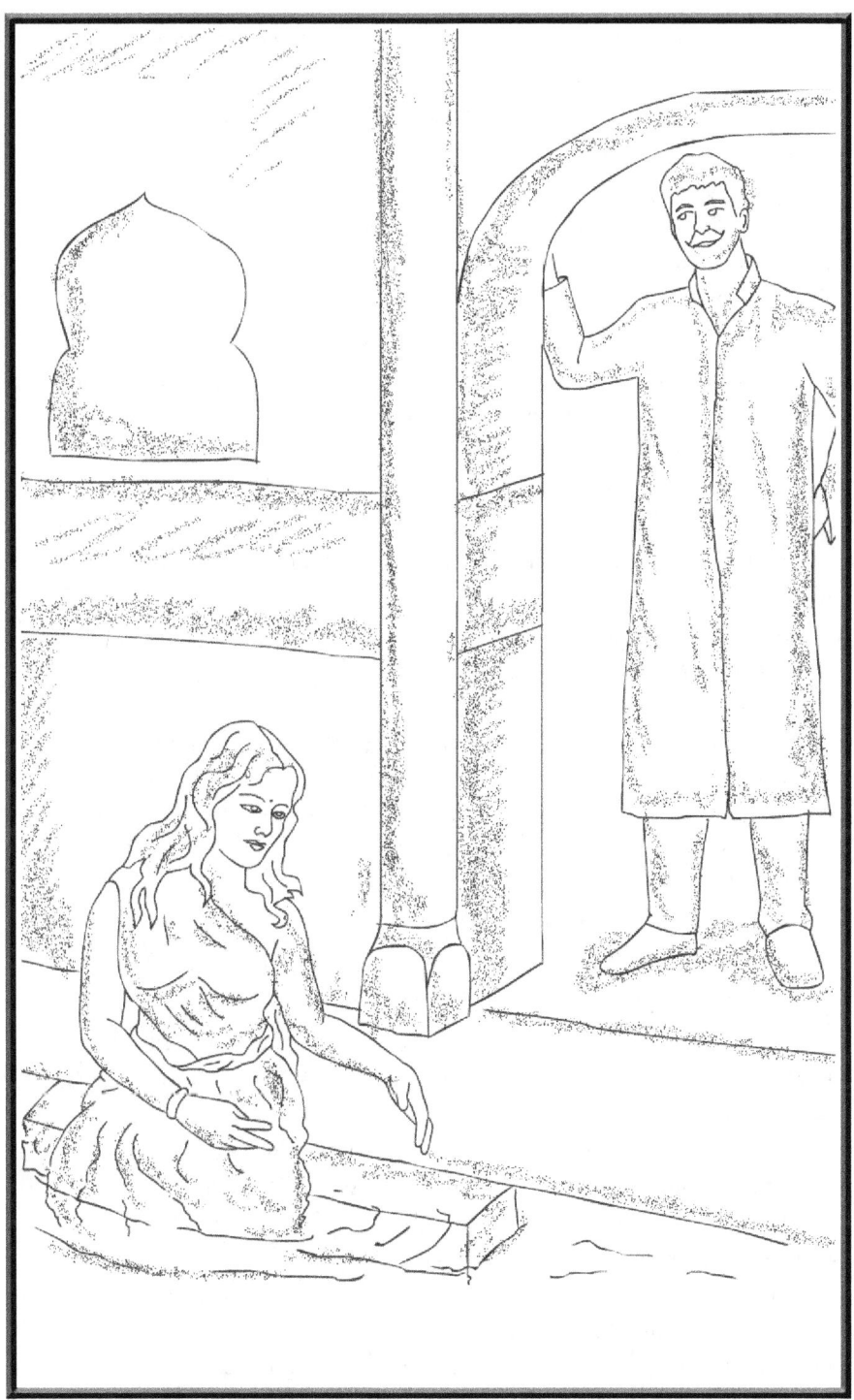

should I raise objections?" Thinking so, he gave her the permission to go as she wished. She left immediately.

Moving alone in that dead darkness of night Madansenā was stopped by a thief, who caught a part of her cloth. He asked, "O Beauty! Who are you? Where are you going?"

She said, "Leave me alone! You have nothing to do with my purpose. I have an urgent work."

The thief said, "How can you get rid of a thief?"

She said, "If you are a thief then take all my ornaments and let me go!"

The thief said, "O Beauty! What have I to do with these stones? You have a moon like face and you are the ornament of the world. I wouldn't spare you."

It was a predicament. She had to tell about herself and her purpose. She requested the thief, "O Gentleman! Please wait for some time. I will return soon after keeping my promise. Be here. I'll come back. I wouldn't break my promise."

The thief thought that she was a woman that respected truth and promises more than anything else. So, he allowed her to go. He stood in shade waiting for her.

She came to Dharmadatta. He was amazed. She narrated the sequence of events and also what she told her husband. He thought for a moment and said patiently, "O Beauty! I'm happy at your truthfulness. But I have nothing to do with a married woman who belongs to someone else. Please return before anyone sees you here."

Madansenā said, "I'll follow it." Saying so, she returned.

On the way she met the thief who was waiting for her. He asked, "O lady! Tell me, what happened with you?"

She repeated her talk. Then the thief said, "If it is so then I too respect truth, and because of that also I release you. Now, you can fearlessly return to your place."

Having been rejected by a once passionate admirer and an unrefined thief who set her free without doing any harm Madansenā happily returned to her husband. She entered the chamber of her husband who was waiting restlessly. He asked, "What happened?"

The newly-wed narrated the whole episode. Samudradatta heard her out carefully. He found her happy, there was no sign of copulation and she had her original brightness. He was sure that although she had gone to keep her promise she saved her virginity and is still pure at heart. He lauded her courage and lived happily with her.

Having finished the story, Vetāla asked the king, "O Emperor! Remember the curse pronounced earlier. Now tell me, who among the three, two businessmen and a thief, greater and whose sacrifice is more valuable?"

Again the king had to break his vow of silence for the fear that his head would break into hundred pieces. He said, "Among them, the thief's sacrifice is greater. The businessmen sacrificed nothing. Their deeds do not come under the category of sacrifice. The husband belonged to a high family. When he came to know that his wife loved another person then how could he have accepted her? So, he allowed her to go. The other businessman left her untouched either out of fear or he lost interest in her with the passage of time. The thief was a sinner and a criminal. His sole interest was in whatever he got during his errand. He left the lady with her ornaments untouched was a sacrifice of his trade for the sake of truth. He is the greatest among them."

Vetāla heard it and vanished from his shoulder, and went to the tree he resided. Without getting bewildered from the supernatural and magical show of Vetāla, the king decided to take him to the Monk, that very night and moved towards the rosewood tree again.

maintained. That is the reason that accountants are part and creature of God.

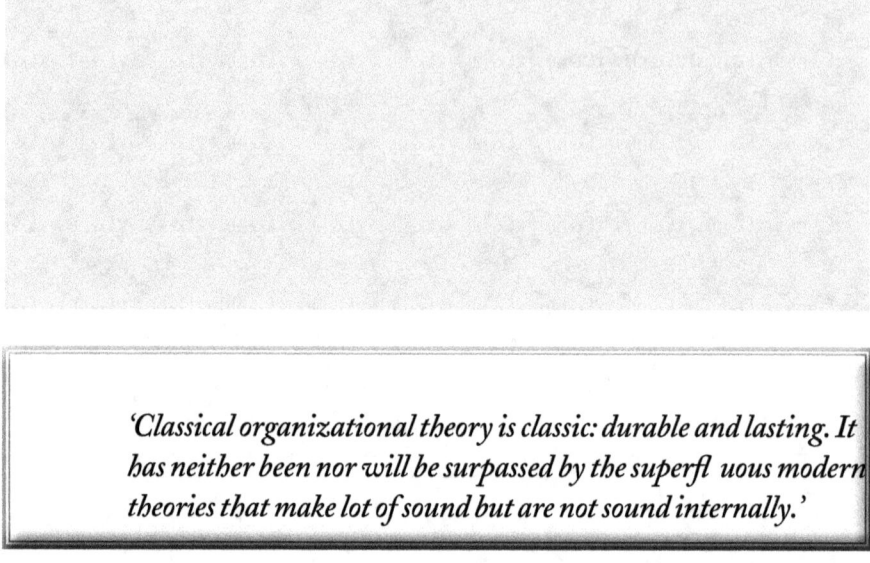

'Classical organizational theory is classic: durable and lasting. It has neither been nor will be surpassed by the superfl uous modern theories that make lot of sound but are not sound internally.'

11

It is necessary for executives to explore true potential;
which increases, decreases and remains substantial
Total achievement at the end counts most, but
It's better to keep doing best, healing up from the initial.

Queens of King Dharmadhwaj

King Vikram Sen reached that rosewood tree again and picked up the corpse with laughing Vetāla in it; put it up on his shoulder and started walking towards the Buddha Monk.

The Vetāla in the dead body said, "O Emperor! You don't realise what you are doing. Yet I'm impressed by your devotion. For this reason, I'm telling you a strange story to remove your tiredness.

In the ancient period King Dharmadhwaj ruled over Ujjaini. He had three loving queens. The first one was Indulekhā; the second was Tārāwali and the third one was Mringānkwati . They were beautiful, pleasant and tender. The king enjoyed their company and lived happily after conquering all the kings and kingdoms in the neighbourhood.

During Spring Season (Basantotasava), the king came to his beautiful garden with his three wives for pleasure. In full passion the king was playing with the hair of queen Indulekhā; a lotus flower decorated over her ears fell in her lap. The flower hit the tendril like tender queen that she screamed in pain and fainted. The King got worried. His servants assisted the queen to regain her consciousness. The queen was immediately treated to fresh water and somehow brought back to her senses. Then the king carried her over to his capital city and hundreds of doctors were called for the treatment of the queen.

By night, King was assured that queen Indulekhā was hale and hearty. So he went to his second queen Tārāwali to spend the night. The king brought the queen to his Chandra Bhawan to enjoy the cool rays of the moon. When the queen was lying on the lap of the king, the rays of the moon started falling directly on the queen through a window.

The queen got up and screamed, "Oh! I'm burning." She left the bed.

The king was amazed and said, "What has happened?"

When he checked her body he found many blisters on it.

The queen said, "The moon rays falling directly on my body have burnt it."

The king was worried to see the queen crying in pain and bearing burning sensations. The King called the servants and got another bed ready with wet lotus leaves for the queen. A thin paste of sandal powder was smeared over the affected parts. The queen felt relieved.

In the meantime, another mishap occurred with the third queen, Mringānkwati who wanted to go to the King. She came out of her palace and started heading towards the King's palace. But in the dead of night, she heard sounds of pestle as if some paddy was being grinded. The force of the sound was so harsh and hard that she cried aloud, "Ah! I'm dead!" saying so she started shaking her hands in fear and sat down there. The servants took her back to her central chamber. She slept on the bed but was weeping. The servants asked, "What has happened?"

They inspected her hands and noticed two hard corn-like tumours on the palm. They rushed to the king and informed him. The King was worried. He rushed to her. She showed both her palms and clarified, "O my master! I heard the sound of pestle that was hitting me hard; as a result these tumours came up on my palms." To relieve the pain sandal paste was applied on her palms. The King then thought about the situation arising from these three incidents in which one of his queens was injured by a lotus flower; another queen burnt up; and mysterious sounds caused tumours on the palms. The tenderness deemed as the symbol of civilization, refinement and high birth has become a disqualification and a curse, the King thought and wandered in the palace courtyard. The King somehow spent that painful night in restlessness.

In the morning, the king called all the physicians who were experts in the treatment of such inflictions and injuries. He asked them to find a permanent cure. After the treatment for a few days, the queens recovered their original prowess and the King spent the rest of his life in pleasure and peace.

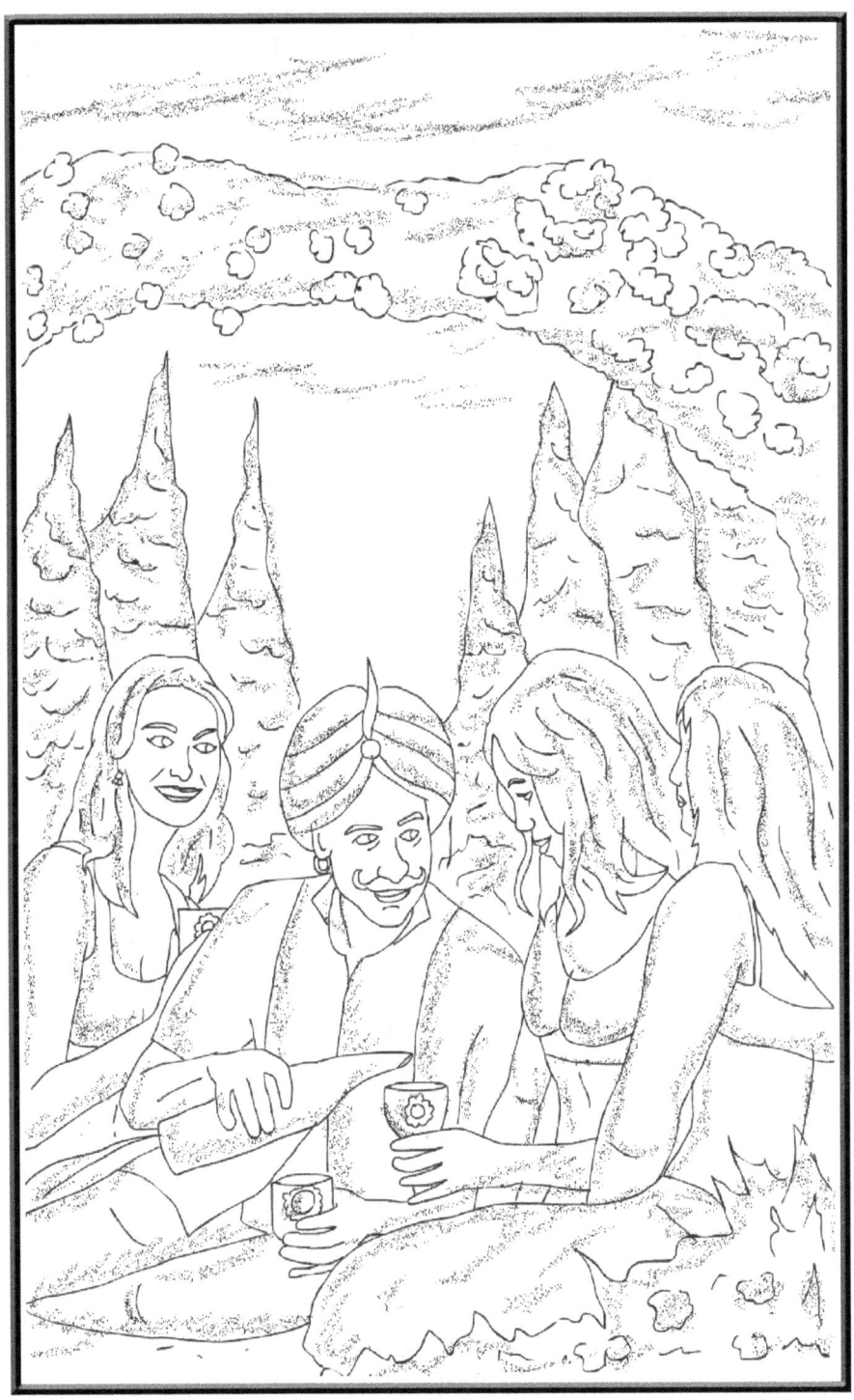

After finishing the story, Vetāla asked, "O Emperor! Who is the most delicate and tender among them?" Vikram answered, "The queen who got tumours after hearing some sounds is most delicate; there was no actual contact of the pestle on her body. There was actual contact with the body of the queen in whose lap the lotus flower fell; and the rays of the moon too touched the body of the other queen."

Vetāla heard it and vanished from his shoulder, and went to the tree where it resided. Without getting bewildered from the supernatural and magical show of Vetāla, the king moved forward to take him to the Monk, that very night.

indicates thefts and scams in the company. One must be conscious

It must be marked that the King took immediate steps to bring

'The use of power may get different responses: resistance; obedience; compliance; conformity; or commitment.'

12

The behaviour shapes the mind wrong or right,
On the hooks that are used and those they bite,
An executive can come clean from disasters
If thinks what is just and does what is right?

King Yashahketu

King Vikram Sen reached that rosewood tree and picked up the human corpse with laughing Vetāla in it and walked briskly but silently towards the Buddha Monk. The Vetāla in the dead body on the shoulders of King Vikram said, "O Emperor! I'm pleased with your patience and quiet attitude. For this very reason, I'm telling you a very interesting story to take out your tiredness."

Once upon a time, a youthful King Yashahketu ruled over the country of Anga. The young, strong and handsome king conquered all enemies. That king had a wise minister named Deerghadarshi. Once, the king passed all responsibilities of the kingdom to the able shoulders of the Minister to indulge in youthful pleasures. He would spend all his time with women in the interior of the palace. He would listen to only their lovely songs full of love. He did not listen to the advice of his friends. He was deeply enjoyed the sights inside curtained windows but would not enjoy the problem ridden tough works of the court. Only Deerghadarshi was bearing that heavy burden of royal responsibilities.

Despite his alertness, rumours were rife that Deergharshi deliberately pushed the king into passions and luxury to enjoy the benefits of royal treasure himself. The minister did not like the scandal. In order to get a way out of the scandalous situation he went to his wife, Medhāwini, and said:

"The king has fallen deep in luxury. I'm doing the best that I'm capable of but the people have started blaming me that I swallowed the kingdom. I'm being defamed. The public satire creates sinful deeds even among the great and pious. Because of such scandals created by a washer man, Lord Rāma, deserted Sitā and exiled her to forest. Now, what should I do?"

The wise wife said, "O Master! Go to the king and on the pretext of pilgrimage request him to allow you to go on pilgrimage for some time. It will kill the scandal immediately and in your absence the king will look after the kingdom. Slowly, in due course he may lose the intensity of his love for luxury. After your return you will get your safe and unblemished post as minister." Scandal should be fought wisely; and if the chief has gone astray he should be brought back to the right track tactfully.

Deerghadarshi accepted the advice wholeheartedly and decided to go on pilgrimage. One day, while discussing matters, the minister with folded hand requested the king, "O King! I have grown old, so I want to go on pilgrimage for some time. Religion is very dear to me."

The king said, "O Mantri! Don't do it. You can show your religiosity through charity. Pilgrimage is not the only way."

The minister said, "O King! In charity the purity of the wealth is essential, while the places of pilgrims always remain pure. One should go on pilgrimage while he has physical health and strength."

But their talk was interrupted by a maid who came and informed that the sun was going in the middle of the pond of sky; that the time of his bath is getting late. Having heard it the king got up and walked inside for his bath. The minister also returned but he was determined to go for the journey. He bowed to the queen and returned. His wife too wanted to accompany him but he stopped her and after making necessary preparations, he went on the voyage.

The minister travelled alone to many distant lands and visited many famous places of pilgrimage. At last, he reached a country called Oudra. He went to a city near the sea. He found a temple of Lord Shiva, he entered its courtyard, performed *poojā* and sat down there. Nidhidatta, a businessman of immense wealth too came there to worship the Lord. He saw the sun-tanned face and dusty body of the traveller sitting there. He closely watched him, saw his sacred thread and thought that he was a sublime Brahmin on pilgrimage. He took him to his residence for hospitality. When he had taken his bath and meal, was at ease, then the merchant asked him, "Who are you? From where have you come? Where will you go?"

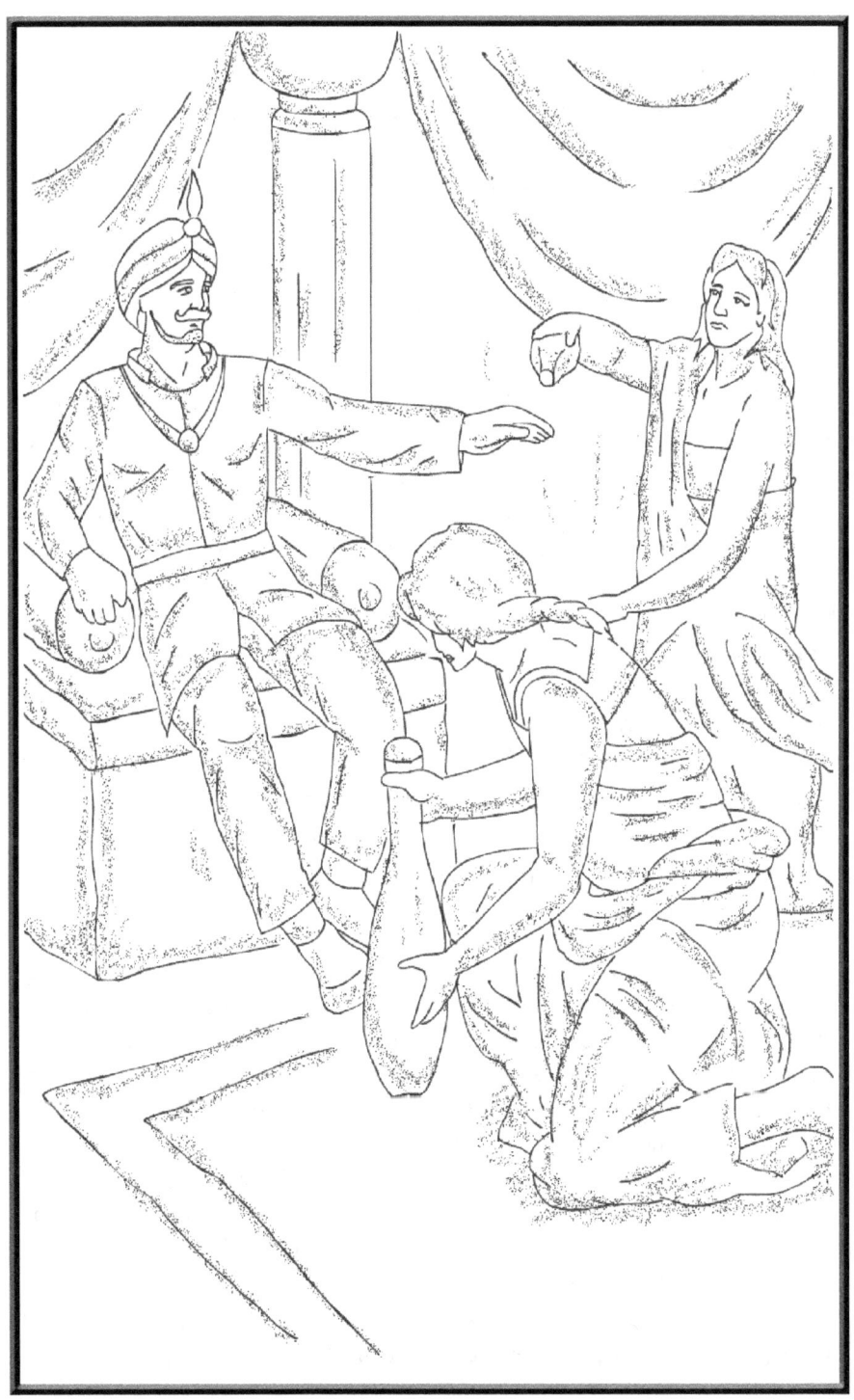

The minister replied, "I'm Deerghadarshi, a Brahmin. I have come on pilgrimage from the country of Anga."

The merchant said, "I'm ready to go to Golden Island for business. You may reside and take rest at this place. You are tired of travelling. After taking adequate rest then you may go to visit other places."

Deerghadarshi heard it and said, "My stay here is quite useless. I would like to accompany you to Golden Island."

The merchant agreed and the minister spent the night there and left the bed very early in the morning. He was ready by the time the others wake up. Then he went with the merchant to the ship and boarded it. While going through that ship. He enjoyed the sight of the turbulent sea. They reached the Golden Island. The merchant, Nidhidatta, completed his business and after sometime they started their return journey.

Then in the sea he saw the Kalpbriksha – a divine tree that gives all green leaves, beautiful boughs and golden brightly glowing stem that was laden with very colourful and attractive flowers. Then he saw a wonderful girl who was extremely beautiful, and was sitting on a bed among the thick branches of the tree. The minister was amazed to see the sight. He could hardly say, 'Oh! What is it?" In the meantime, she took up a musical instrument in her hands and started playing it and started singing a very sweet and meaningful song:

Yena yet karmabeejamuptam sa nischitam tatphalam bhungakte;
Purvakritam hi karmam vidhinā api anyathā kartum na shakyate.

$\Big($ Whatever seeds of deeds one sows he must face its effects.
Even the creator can't change the effects of the deeds done earlier. $\Big)$

That divine girl of sublime beauty sang in this way and when the song was over she went inside the deep sea along with the tree as she had risen from it. The minister could not take his eyes off her. When she had vanished then he thought: Has the sea been like this from the earliest period? No, had it been so, then how did the Goddess Laxmi, the Moon, Dhanwantari and Pārijāta come out of it? When the navigators saw him so amazed at the unusual and wonderful sight they informed him. "O Gentleman! It is a very usual affair. We have seen this beautiful girl many times at this particular place. She comes out of the sea, completes her song and returns to the sea. You have seen it for the first time."

The minister heard them but he could not get a plausible reason for it. He returned to the shore with the merchant. He stayed with him happily for many days. Then one day he asked Nidhidatta, the merchant, "I have stayed with your happily for quite a long time. Now I want to return home." The merchant tried to stop him but he was adamant and giving thanks and wishing them great prosperity he started his return journey.

After travelling through many countries the minister reached his own country, Angadesha. The secret agents of the king Yashahketu were looking for him. They saw him and informed the king about his arrival. The king was tired of long separation from the minister. He hurried out to the end of the city to welcome the minister. It was a happy reunion. He embraced the minister that had sun-tanned face and dusty body. He requested the minister to get fresh and take rest.

When the minister was fresh and at ease then the king said, "O Mantri! Why did you leave us and gave so much of pain to your body and mind? It may be the wish of Goddess Shakti. Who can say anything with surety? What turned you to go for such difficult pilgrimage? Now, tell us where did you go and what did you see? What was new in it?"

Then the minister narrated his journey in short but the wonderful incident in the sea when he saw the divine girl with sublime beauty in detail. She was like the essence of all the three worlds and sang that meaningful song coming out of the sea on the Kalpabriksha.

The king heard it and was full of passion for that rare beauty. He thought that his life had no meaning without her. One day, in solitude he informed the minister, "O Mantri! I will sure go there to see that beauty. Otherwise, I would die. I would bow to the future happening and follow the way that you have described. Neither you should stop me, nor follow me. I shall secretly go alone. In my absence, you would look after my kingdom. Don't go against my orders. I give you the oath of my life."

The king shrugged off the resistance of the minister on the adventure but saw him off from there. The minister Deerghadarshi was almost always serious and sad even during grand festivals. Good ministers cannot take rest when their master is immersed neck-deep in luxury and others passions.

Then, one day, the king Yashahketu, placed all the responsibility on the minister Deerghdarshi, changed his dress, became a yogi in penance and left the capital city for that magical destination deep down the sea. On the way, he met a Muni named Kushi. He calculated his mission and advised him, "Board the ship of the merchant called, Laxmidatta and go to the designated place in the sea. You will get the desired lady. So, have patience and go peacefully."

The king heard the sage and was pleased to hear the forecast of his success. He bowed to him, saluted and happily moved on. He crossed over many countries, rivers and mountains and came to the sea. At the bank he befriended Laxmidatta Merchant. The merchant saw the celestial sign of wheels on his feet. So he was humble towards the king. The king boarded his ship and travelled towards his destination.

At the middle of the sea, suddenly the girl with sublime beauty appeared sitting among the branches of the Kalpabriksha. The king looked at her as a *Chakore* bird looks lovingly towards the moon. In the meantime she started singing the song that meant that the fruit of good or bad deeds are to be tasted by everyone; what one has done earlier, even the creator can't change its fruit. Whatever and wherever one has to get or lose something, it has to happen. Nothing can change it. That person is brought to that place by the force of his prior actions and their resultant effects.

The king stood still, looking directly towards the girl that was giving the information regarding the happenings that are fixed; and are to happen. The king prayed to the sea, "O Sea! Treasure House of Jewels! I salute thee! You enchanted Lord Vishnu with equal beauty, Laxmi! So, I have come in your shelter. I salute thee; fulfill my desire!"

When the king was praising the sea and praying to him, the girl dipped inside the sea along with the tree. The king dropped his body in her direction. The merchant Laxmidatta thought; "The person who had dived into the sea, has died. We must go behind him even if he dies in the sea." Just when he was ready to jump into the sea an aerial sound cautioned him, "Don't try to be a daredevil. Don't worry about him. He wouldn't die. The recluse is none other than the king Yashahketu. He has come for that girl, as she was his wife in the previous life. With her he would return to his country Angadesha.

Inside the sea, Yashahketu suddenly saw a divine city. He was wonderstruck to see bright jewelled pillars; walls glowing like gold; palaces that had windows decorated with pearls; ponds had the stairs constructed with a variety of stones; with gardens beautified with the trees that fulfilled all the wishes. The city projected all sorts of prosperity. He searched each house one by one but could not find his beloved. At last he reached a high palace that was made up of jewels. Slowly he opened the door, entered inside and saw a girl sleeping on a bed of jewels. She had covered her whole body in a shawl.

The King became suspicious, "Is she that very girl?" He eagerly uncovered her face. He saw his desired girl. It was like an oasis in summer to a thirsty traveller. He was pleased like such a person. She also opened her eyes and saw the handsome young man full of sublime and refined qualities. She hurriedly left her bed. She welcomed the king, and looked at his feet as if she was worshipping the feet with her lotus eyes.

Slowly she started speaking, "O humble soul! Who are you? How have you entered this unfathomable depth of the sea? You have all the qualities of a king. Why have you taken the garb of a recluse? O Gentle soul! If you are kind to me then tell me."

The king heard her and happily said, "O Beauty! I'm Yashahketu, the king of Angadesha. I heard about you from a faithful person. I thought that I must see and meet you. I took this garb only for you. I left my kingdom and have come up to you by following the directions given to me. Now, tell me who are you." She expressed shyness and love towards him. She lovingly said, "There was a prosperous Vidyādhar (Genie) named Mriganksena. You can treat me as his daughter Mrigankawati. Because of some reason my father deserted me. He left me alone here and went out with all the persons of the city. I don't know the reason. That is why I'm living alone in this deserted city. I often go out from this uninhabited city on the Kalpabriksha to sing the song of destiny."

The king remembered the forecast of the Muni. He said such loving things in loving manner that she was intoxicated and agreed to marry him at that very moment. But she laid a condition, "O My Master! Every month on the 4th and 8th day of both the fortnights I would go somewhere. You should not try to stop me or see me. There is a definite reason behind it."

The king accepted the condition saying, "I will abide by it."

Then, the king married her according to the marriage rules of the Nymphs and lived there happily with his wife Mrigānkawati. The king had forgotten everything and was deeply engrossed in the most satisfying physical pleasure. One day, she said, "O my husband! The fourth day of the month has come. Please wait here. I will go out for some work. During my absence please don't enter that house made up of crystals and don't dive in this pond. If you will do that then immediately you would be transported to your country."

Giving such instructions she went out of the city with his permission. The king was eager to know the secret. So, he took out his sword and fearlessly followed her. Outside the city he saw a fabulous and dreadful demon coming. His shadow fell like darkness. His mouth was like a cave. His body was like a hill. He came towards Mringānkwati and roared with a terrific sound, caught her in his mouth and swallowed her. It was unbearable for the king. Out of anger he rushed fast like a cobra with fresh-shed skin and cut off the head of the Demon.

The king was blind in love with his wife. He was aggrieved at her loss. He could not move after killing the Demon. He felt black clouds around him. But Mringānkwati, tearing off the body of the Demon, came out alive, safe and full like the idol of bright moon. He saw her and felt that he had won over the problem. He called her, "Come darling, come" and rushed towards her and embraced her. He asked, "O darling! What was it? Was it a dream or an illusion?"

That Genie has got the knowledge of her past. She now remembered everything. She thought over it and then answered, "O my husband! It was neither a dream nor an illusion. It was the effect of the curse showered on me by my father, the king of Genie. My father, the Genie king Mringānksena, had many sons but he loved me so much that he would not take his meal in my absence; and often I was so much engrossed in worshipping Lord Shiva that I was often late for the meal. On every 14th day of each fortnight I used to come to this lonely place for worshipping Gauri.

Once, on the 14th day I came here and went on worshipping Gauri for hours and unfortunately spent the whole day in it. That day, my father was angry over me as he had not taken his meal because of my absence. Out of anger, he did not eat anything throughout the day. During the night I went before him with bowed hand as a criminal. He did not feel love at that time. I had committed a crime. For one thing I would not have sacrificed the other. I should have returned at the right time and after taking meal I could have resumed worshipping. But I was not conscious towards my duties and responsibilities.

My father thought over it and punished me with a curse, 'Out of disrespect you forgot this hungry man for the whole day long. So, every month on both the 8th and 14th days you would come to worship him with love for Shiva; then *Kritrānta Santrās* Demon would swallow you. You would come out after tearing his heart. You will forget this curse and the pain of being swallowed; and will remain here alone.' When I repeatedly requested for the release from the curse, then after thinking for sometime he announced the end of the curse. 'When Yashahketu, the king of Angadesha would come to you as your husband and would kill the demon when he would see that you are being swallowed by him; then you would be freed from the curse, and remember everything, including the unique powers of the Genie. And with it he also punished himself for excess indulgence in love for children. It was a two-way curse. He left me alone here and went up on the Nishadha mountain along with all the people of the city. Since then I'm living here alone. As the effect of the curse is gone because of your valour so, I feel that it is the day to go to my father on the Nishadha mountain. Now, I would regain my previous status. It was agreed in the curse. So, I will go back to my father. It is up to you to live here or return to your country. You are free to take the decision."

The king heard all and requested her to be with him for the next seven days. He requested, "O Beauty! Don't go for seven days. O shapely figure! I would spend my days in your pleasant company during that period. Then you can go to the place of your father and I would return to my kingdom."

She said, "I would obey your order, abide by it and follow it." They spent the six days in that lovely garden of pure water and big swans. On the 7th day, the king deliberately, in a planned way took his beloved wife to the pond that was the way to his country. He embraced her there and in that embrace he jumped into the pond with her and came out from the middle of his pond in his garden and in his kingdom.

The gardeners saw the king. They happily informed the minister Deerghadarshi. He came with the relatives and courtiers to welcome the king and the queen. They touched the feet of the king to show respect. They greeted them and happily with music and dance they ceremoniously performed the rituals of the entrance in house with wife. The minister saw her and thought, "O! How this king got possession of the lady that I saw for a moment as lightning and then vanished. Whatever the God has written as destiny, will come to be true, howsoever strange, it may appear." That prime minister and other people kept on thinking about the extremely beautiful and royal queen.

The week of the promise came to an end. Now, she thought of returning to her old status. She tried to remember the knowledge of Genie but she could not remember the science of flying into air. She was very sad. The king saw her and asked, "Why are you so sad? My darling, tell me."

The Genie queen said to the king, "I remained tied to your loving arms even up to seven days after getting free from the curse. It took off my science and the art of flying."

The king thought that the Genie has become human now. He was so pleased with it that he arranged a great function and feast. The minister Deerghadarshi could not tolerate it. He went back to his bed during the night but his heart burst and he died of heart failure. The king took control of the kingdom. Along with Mringānkwati the king Yasghahketu happily ruled over Angadesha for quite a long period.

After finishing the story, Vetāla asked, "O Emperor! The prosperity of the master affected the heart of the minister. It burst out and he died. What is the reason behind it? Is it that he himself could not get that divine beauty or is it that he wanted to control the kingdom that was spoilt because of the return of the king? If you would avoid the answeer knowingly then you would fall from your *dharma* and your head will break up into hundred pieces."

Vikram answered, "O Yogiswar! It is a shame to think like that about the minister of noble nature and conduct. These two possibilities can never be true to such an honest and sincere minister. The minister must have thought in a different way; that when the king was infatuated in woman of general category then he took no notice of the kingly duties but now he is infatuated by a woman of divine beauty. What will happen to the kingdom? Despite best efforts the problems are growing day by day instead of solving them. He thought over it so hard that his heart crashed. I feel like that."

Vetāla heard it and vanished from his shoulder, and went to the tree where he resided. Without getting bewildered from the supernatural and magical show of Vetāla, the king decided to take him to the Monk.

Why Smart Executives Fail

ce.

make him take needed interest.

rous.

under grip.

'Authority is the power to utilise discretion in making decisions to be followed by others.'

13

Motivation in an executive will not remain the same
In production, distribution, management or security game,
He usually gets the desired result in an effective way
With intelligence and diligence earlier, and latter on fame

Lāwanyawati, the Wife of Hariswāmi

King Vikram Sen reached that rosewood tree again and picked up the human corpse with laughing Vetāla on it. Taking the dead body on his shoulder the King walked towards the Buddha Monk. The Vetāla in the dead body on the shoulders of King Vikram said, "O Emperor! Now, listen to a very short story."

There was a very ancient city called Varanasi where a Brahmin, named Devaswāmi lived. He was respected by the king. The Brahmin was very rich and had a son called Hariswāmi who had an extremely beautiful wife, named Lāwanyawati.

One night, Hariswāmi was sleeping with his beloved wife on the roof under the cool and soothing rays of the moon, after making love. At that very night a young Vidyādhar (Genie), named Madanvega who used to travel in the sky passed through that roof. Seeing the incarnation of beauty sleeping with her husband, the Genie could not control his love and passion for her. He lifted her up in sleep and eloped with her through the aerial route.

After some time, Hariswāmi woke up and not finding his beloved wife, he screamed, "Where has she gone? Is she angry with me? Or is she hiding somewhere to watch my reaction and make a mockery of me?" Many ideas flashed into his mind. He searched her at every possible place: on the roof, in the rooms, in the balcony, in the rooms at downstairs, kitchen and at other places. But he did not find her.

The worried husband came out and looked in the garden but his beloved wife was nowhere. He became desperate. Out of passionate agony he started crying loudly: "Ah! Moon – faced beloved! Where are you? Ah my beloved Lāwanyawati! Where have you gone? You were equal to this moonlit night in beauty so out of jealousy the night has hidden you somewhere! Where are you? The moon that used to give me pleasure with its soothing rays is now burning me like hot embers? It is giving pain like the poisoned arrows."

Hariswāmi spent that night weeping in pain for his wife but the pain of separation failed to heal up. In the morning the sun wiped out the darkness from the world but not from the heart, mind and life of Hariswāmi. His pitiable weeping and painful cry increased hundred folds. His relatives tried their best to console him but he had lost his only and the best possession. He was not satisfied and could not get contentment. He was in a half mad state. He would go to different places and remember the incidents and the pleasant moments they had together: "I had sat with her here! We had taken bath here! Here she finished her makeup! It is here that we enjoyed and spent our leisure!" He kept on telling such things and crying bitterly for his lost beloved wife.

His friends, brothers and relative gave him solace by telling, "Why are you killing yourself? She is not dead as yet so, she must be somewhere. In place of weeping for her at this place, search for her at other places. There is no wealth greater than patience. You can get her back if you search her patiently." It gave him the right logic.

After a few days he came to his senses and decided to give away everything that he had to Brahmins and go to visit pilgrimages and wipe the sins out. If and when the sins are wiped out then there is a chance that he can get his beloved back. He thought like that and then rethink about his decision and do accordingly.

The next day he arranged a feast open to all. Many different types of delicious dishes were cooked; the Brahmin and the poor were fed well and he gave all his wealth in charity to them. He took only a bit of wealth with him and went out for pilgrimage.

The summer came. The sun grew hot. It was very hot lion-like rays that started burning and wiping out the greenery from the fields. The wind too grew hotter being touched by the hot breathing of the lovers in separation. It blew hot and burnt the travellers on their way. The ponds dried out. They

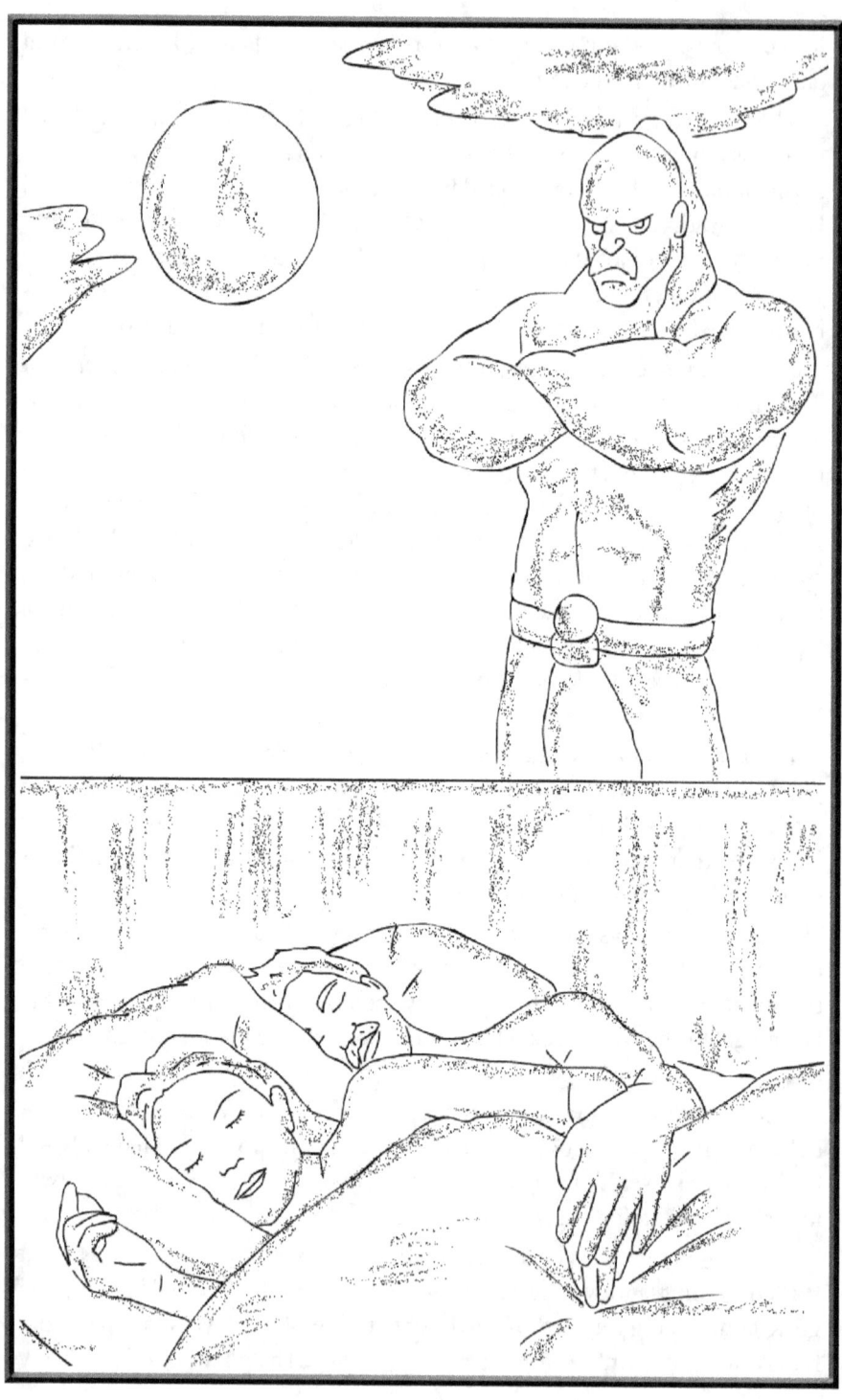

became muddy first then cracks appeared as the burning rays evaporated water. The birds cried when they found the trees and their leaves drying and withering. They expected the spring but looked like separated from it. Nature teaches patience and endurance.

During such a hot summer, one day Hariswāmi reached a village, burnt by the hot sun, aggrieved at the separation from the beloved wife, thirsty and hungry, tired out of travelling. He was in search of food and shelter.

He saw Brahmins taking meal at the house of a Brahmin, named Padmanābha. He went there silently and stood at the very gate motionless holding the frame of the door with one hand and back touching its panel. The Brahmin had performed some *yagya* and had arranged feast for the Brahmins. The kind and compassionate wife of that Brahmin thought, "O hunger is terrific! It belittles all! He is someone who needs food. He is standing with his heads down. He seems to have come from some distant place. He has not taken bath and is weak. He deserves food."

Thinking so, that sincere housewife took a pot full of milk mixed with butter and sugar and gave it to Hariswāmi and said, "There is a pond there. Please sit there and take it."

Hariswāmi took the pot and said, "As you wish." He went to the pond and placed the pot under a banyan tree before entering the pond to wash his hands and legs.

In the meantime, an eagle came with a black snake caught in its talons and sat on the tree just above the pot of milk. It started eating the snake. At that time saliva mixed with poison came out of the mouth of the snake and dropped down in the pot.

Hariswāmi washed his hands and feet, cleansed his mouth and returned to the place where he kept the pot. He had no knowledge of what had happened during his absence. He was hungry and ready to take his meal. He finished it in no time. But immediately he felt the burning sensation of poison. "Oh God! The sweet dish has turned to be poison for me." Saying so and staggering, he somehow walked up to the house of the Brahmin that had performed the *yagya*. He said there, "O Brahmini! Your food has changed into poison for me! Be quick! Call someone who can take out the effect of the poison. Otherwise, you will be guilty of killing a Brahmin."

That sincere housewife exclaimed, "How did it happen?" She was restless. She called the person for his treatment. But before he was taken care of and administered medicine, the eyes of Hariswāmi turned upside down and he collapsed.

The Brahmin that had performed the *yagya* was very angry with his wife. Though, she was innocent, she had done nothing wrong, she was sincere, hospitable, kind and compassionate, yet she was exiled. She decided to go for penance and she moved towards one pilgrimage centre.

After finishing the story, Vetāla asked, "O Emperor! Out of the snake, the eagle and the wife of the Brahmin, who gave food in charity, who is responsible for the death of the Brahmin? It was debated in the court of Dharmarāja but it remained undecided. Now, O the Ruler of Kings! You should say who is to be blamed for the killing of the Brahmin? Remember, the curse is hanging there if you tell a lie and know the truth."

Vikram again had to break his silence. He answered honestly and logically, "Who is to be blamed for the killing of the Brahmin? The snake was enslaved. He was not free and his enemy was eating him. He can't be blamed for Brahmahatyā. The hungry eagle also did not see anything. It was trying to satisfy its hunger. It cannot be blamed. The couple or one of the couple, that fed a guest that came suddenly, also can't be blamed because they were performing *yagya* and doing something religious. So, they are not to be blamed. I think, he would be blamed for Brahmahatyā who would blame any of these three for the death of the Brahmin without thinking about it." After telling it, the king became silent again.

Vetāla heard it and vanished from his shoulder, and went to the tree where he resided. Without getting bewildered from the supernatural and magical show of Vetāla, the king decided to take him to the Monk, that very night. He followed Vetāla.

management, change management refers to a project management process

Linda Ackerman Anderson, author of *Beyond Change Management* them.

before the commencement of another season. If the products are authorities to be conscious and do necessary checking before

'Strategy is a plan: known to some, unknown to many; to achieve the changing goals fi xed earlier by least active personnel.'

14

Veerketu and Ratnawati

With determination, King Vikram Sen reached the rosewood tree and picked up the human corpse with laughing Vetāla on it, and walked silently towards the Buddha Monk.

The Vetāla began his story with an introduction, "O Emperor! You don't realize what you are doing. Yet I am impressed by your courage, devotion and constant effort. For this reason, I'm telling a short story to take away your tiredness".

The ancient city of Ayodhyā was ruled by a valiant king named Veerketu. During his regime a rich merchant named Ratnadatta lived there. His wife Nandyanti propitiated the gods and gave birth to a daughter Ratnawati who had all good qualities. But she hated men. Many sought her hand for marriage but she refused and warned that if she was married by force, she would sacrifice her life. Being the one and only daughter, the parents too did not take the risk of discussing her marriage.

In the meantime, a daring thief was creating havoc in the city. The city guards were unable to catch him. One day, the aggrieved citizens requested the King to liberate the city from the thief. The King assured immediate action. Though he put detectives on the prowl of the thief; the king Veerketu himself decided to keep a tab in the night and catch him at any cost. The King went in disguise and roamed the streets. One night, the King saw a

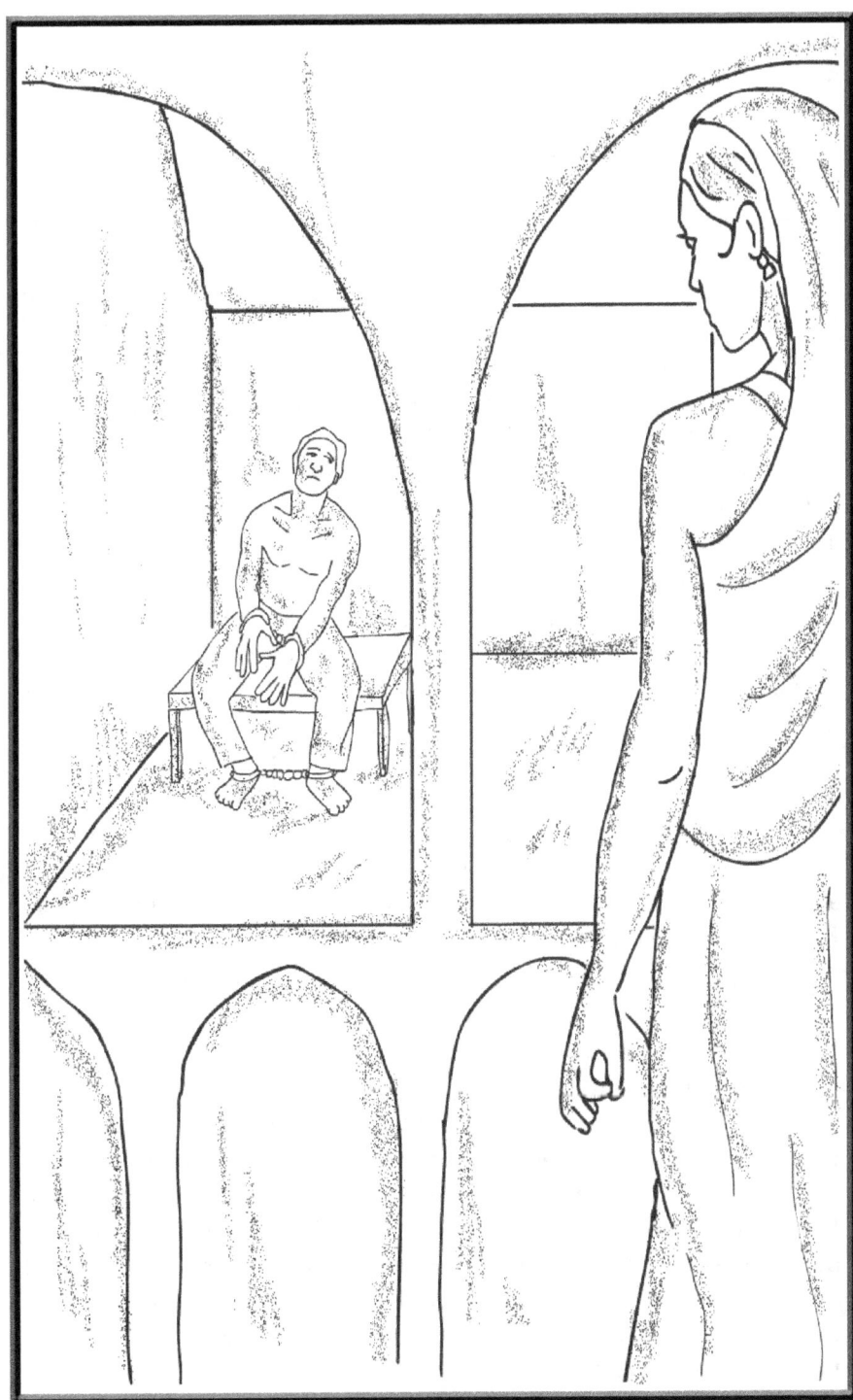

person stealthily climbing a boundary wall. The King went over to him. The thief shouted, "Who are you?" The King replied immediately, "I'm a thief."

The thief was pleased to hear it and said, "Good luck! You are a friend. Please come to my place, so that I can show some hospitality like a friend." The King accepted the invitation and accompanied the thief. They entered a dense forest and finally reached a palace-like building. The king entered that abode of luxury. The thief requested the King to sit there and went inside. In the meantime, a maidservant entered the room and said, "O Gentleman! That thief is a sinner and may kill you. So please run away immediately."

The King returned to his palace and went back with his army and attacked the thief's abode. The thief came out with a sword and fought against the king's soldiers valiantly. He butchered many soldiers and defeated the army. Finally the King himself took on him and defeated him. The King proclaimed death sentence to the thief. The death penalty entailed chopping off his head in the morning at the place for execution.

As the thief was being ushered into the designated place for execution, Ratnawati was watching him from the roof of her palace. The thief was bleeding from his wounds and the body was smeared in dust. Ratnawati felt attracted to him and immediately rushed to her father and announced the decision, "O Father! I have accepted the thief as my husband. He is being led to the place of execution. Please save him. If not then I will die for him."

It was a tough order for the father. The merchant tried hard to change the mind of his only daughter. But she was adamant. So, he rushed to the King and requested him to take all his wealth and free the thief. But once the King had pronounced his decision, it was not possible to retract.

The father returned empty handed. Ratnawati too was adamant and got ready to go to the place of execution with the sole purpose of immolation. She was determined to die with the dead body of the person she had now selected as her husband.

The parents and relatives tried hard to dissuade her but she rejected all pleadings. In bridal makeup she reached the place of execution. A crowd also gathered there. The thief also saw the beautiful girl before execution. He wept for sometime then laughed and was killed as per royal orders. The body was taken off the altar. Ratnawati sat on a pyre with the dead body and the fire was about to be lit. Then Lord Shiva's aerial voice announced, "O Sincere wife! I'm satisfied with your devotion towards this self-selected husband! Ask for blessings!"

She bowed to Lord Shiva and said, "O God! Please bless my childless father with hundred sons so that he may not think of dying after me as he would become childless."

God replied sky, "O Sincere wife! Your wish is granted! Your father will get hundred sons! But it's not for you! For such a courageous and devotee lady this blessing is not enough! Ask something for yourself!"

She prayed again, "O God! If you are pleased with me then this husband of mine should regain life and always remain religious." It was granted.

Merchant Ratnadatta happily accepted his daughter and the son-in-law and returned to his residence. He arranged a grand feast and celebration. The King was conveyed the message of Lord Shiva. The King appointed the thief as the Commander of his army for showing exemplary courage while fighting against the king's army. The thief too changed his habits and turned religious. He married Ratnawati, and lived happily ever after.

After finishing the story, Vetala asked, "O Emperor! why did the thief weep to see the girl and know about her that she had come with her father to the place of execution with the sole purpose to sacrifice herself?"

Vikram answered, "The thief wept as he thought that he could not be free from the debt of the merchant friend. He thought that the woman had a very flickering, unstable mind and hence he laughed at it."

Vetala heard it and vanished from his shoulder, and went to the tree, his abode. Without getting bewildered at the supernatural show of Vetala, the King decided to take him to the Monk, that very night.

mantra

taken other things out.

> "Balance, control, hope, faith and diligence are inherent traits of all successful leaders including Kings, MDs and CEOs"

15

The Story of Princess Shashiprabhā

King Vikram Sen again reached that rosewood tree and picked up the human corpse and started his resolute walk towards the Buddha Monk. The Vetāla in the dead body said; "O Emperor! I'm telling you a short story to take out your tiredness."

In the kingdom of Napal, there was a city called Shivapur. In the ancient period, King Yashahketu ruled there. He gave all responsibilities of the kingdom to his wise minister Pragyā Sāgar and led a luxurious life in the company of his dear queen Chandraprabha. The queen gave birth to a beautiful daughter called Shashiprabhā. She was growing up as a young woman; one day in the spring season, she went to a temple with friends and families.

Manahswāmi – a young son of a Brahmin also came there. He saw Shashiprabha trying to pluck flowers in the temple garden with one of her breasts jutting towards him. It raised his passion. He thought, "Is she *Rati* (the wife of the God of Love) who is collecting the flowers gifted by Spring?" The Princess too caught him looking at her passionately. She thought of him as Cupid in physical form. She too was enchanted by his look; forgot collecting flowers and lost herself in love fantasies.

They stood there like the still figures in a photograph; suddenly they heard a cry, "Oh! Oh! Ah! Ah!" What has happened? Both of them were eager to know it. They raised their heads and tried to look out. It was a big mad elephant ready to attack the princess.

Her friends and servants ran away. Manahswāmi acted swiftly; ran fast towards Shashiprabhā, caught her up in his arms and drew her away from the angry elephant. Her body came very close to him. She was shy and filled up with a different emotion.

When the princess returned to the palace, she felt a burning-sensation inside caused by her own heat of intense physical passion. The young Brahmin followed her to the palace. When she entered her abode, the young man thought, "I can't dare to live even for a moment without her. I feel that, Shri Mooladeva, the Dhurta Guru who is expert in *gutkā* and *tābeeja* (magical pills that intoxicate the desired man or woman) is the only way out for me." After spending that night in anguish the next morning he reached Guru Mooladeva's place and explained his problem and expressed the wish to get the girl as his partner. The Guru promised him help. Then that clever master took one magical pill himself and became an old Brahmin; and gave another magical pill to Manahswāmi and changed him into a beautiful girl. Then he took the 'girl' to the King; and requested: "Oh Emperor, I have only one son. I have begged this girl for him from a distant land but my son has run away to some other place. I am going to search him out. Till my return, please keep this girl in your service and provide her security."

The King agreed. Immediately the king called his daughter Shashiprabhā and instructed her, "O Putri! Keep this girl in your palace and place her bed by yours for security reasons."

Thus Manahswāmi, the Brahmin's son in the garb of a girl was brought to Shashiprabhā's palace. He became very friendly to the Princess. One night, he asked the Princess, "O dear friend! Why are you getting pale every day? Why are you losing your glow so fast? Why are you aggrieved like a separated lover?."

The Princess sighed and said, "Once I had gone to worship the God during the festivals of spring. I was in the garden plucking flowers. There I saw a handsome young man who looked like a moon out of fog. His appearance made me passionate. In the meantime, a wild elephant came charging on me. I was in a spot. The servants had run away. That Brahmin lifted me up in his arms and took me away from the danger."

The heart of Manahswāmi welled up with great pleasure as he listened to the nectar like words of the Princess. His ears delighted. He felt fully satisfied. Now, he knew that the Princess too is in love with him. He decided that it was the right time to declare that he was that original lover.

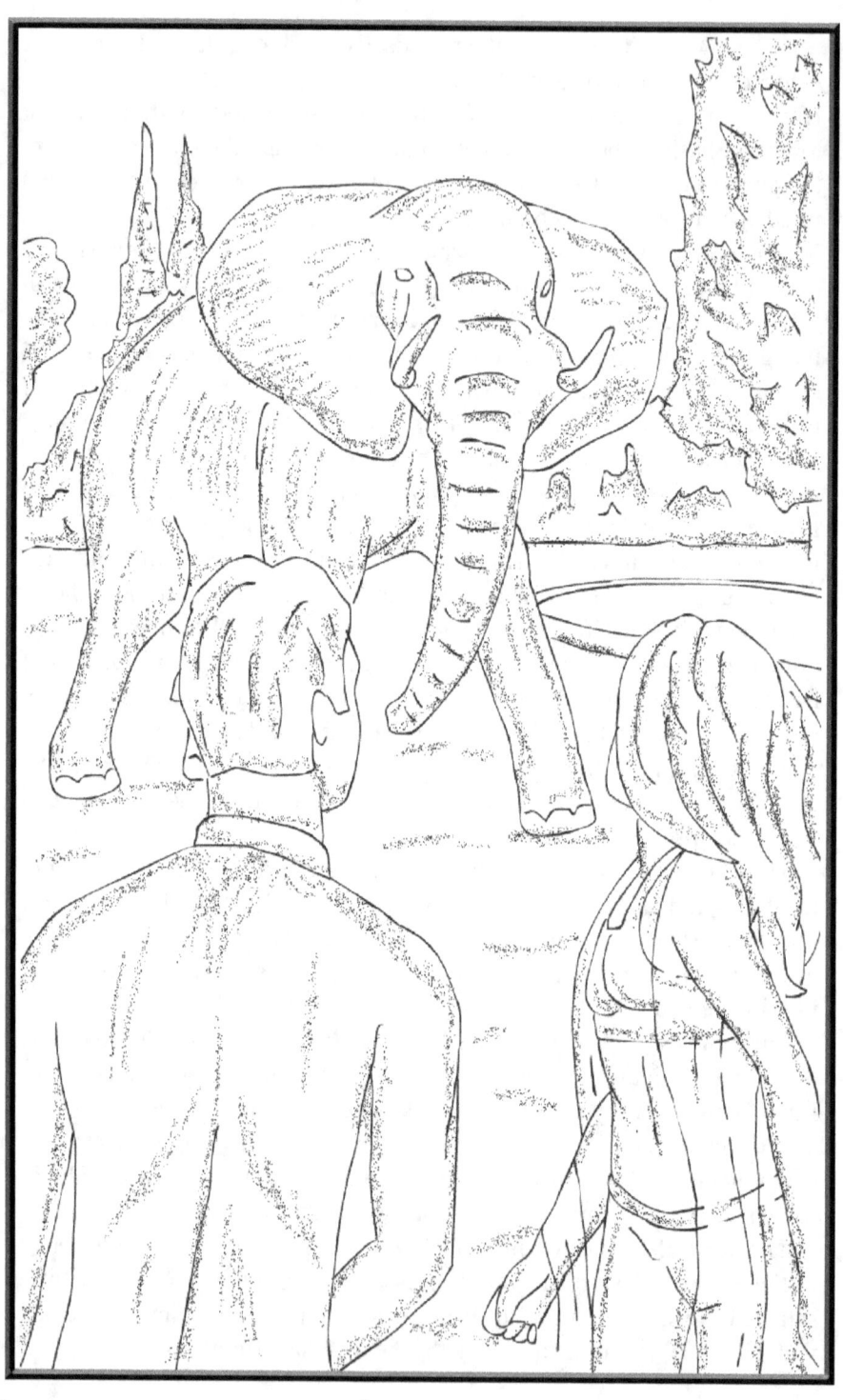

Having decided like that Manahswāmi took off the magical pill from his mouth and again became the original lover of the Princess and said to her, "O Beauty! I'm that very person whom you have enslaved. I have come to you as a girl out of uncontrollable passion. I'm burning in the fire of physical desire. Please cool me down with you tender, pleasant and loving look."

Shashiprabhā was filled up with wonder, shyness, and love. They decided to solemnise the marriage according to customs of the nymphs or *Gandhava vivāha*. They performed the rituals and started living secretly like husband and wife. Manahswāmi had a dual role to play. During the day he would put the pill inside his mouth and turn into a girl; and during the night he took the pill out of his mouth to turn into a man again to enjoy the lovely Princess.

Time passed. The brother-in-law of King Yashahketu married off his daughter Mringākdattā to the son of Prgyāsāgar, who was the minister of king Yashahketu. Along with the Princess, the disguised girl also had attended the marriage. The son of Pragyāsāgar saw her and fell for her. Although, he was married to Mrigānkdattā, he cried for that disguised girl and fainted. The passion of physical pleasure had hit him hard and he lost self control. His worried father consoled him and he went to the king and informed him. It was obvious that he would become mad permanently or he would die soon.

The king was in a fix. If the son dies, the minister would also die. It will be the end of the stability of his kingdom. On the other hand the girl is under his safe custody. He cannot dare to give her to other person. The people suggested that the son of the minister must be saved now.

When the Brahmin returns and demands his daughter in law some other way out can be sought. Thinking thus he accepted the proposal and agreed to marry the girl under his custody to the son of the minister.

When the date and time of the marriage was fixed, the disguised girl put forth some pre-conditions, "O Emperor! You are giving a girl to another that was brought for yet another person. You are the king. You can do it. It is up to you to think of religious or irreligious act. But I would marry on one condition that I would not be forcibly brought to bed by my husband till he returns from pilgrimage for six months. Otherwise, you can treat me as dead."

The king explained the pre-conditions for marriage to the son of the minister and advised him to go on a pilgrimage for six months. The marriage was solemnised. The disguised girl was brought to the house of the minister. She was asked to live with the existing wife of the husband who went on a pilgrimage. The disguised girl started living in the same room with her and shared bed with her. They also took meals together.

They lived like that for some days. One night, when the servants were sleeping, Mringānkdattā requested the disguised girl, "I am not feeling sleepy. Please tell me a story."

The disguised girl told a very long story of the parents of Pururwā. She said, "In ancient times, there was a king name Ilā in the dynasty of the sun (Suryabansh). He was cursed by Pārvati and became a girl that had the enchanting beauty. Budha, (Mercury), the son of Moon who lived in a beautiful garden called Nandanvana, fell in love with her. They were united together. Because of their union a son name Pururwā was born to them." She finished the story and cunningly concluded, "O dear friend! Often it happens that by the orders of the gods a man is changed into a woman or a woman is changed into a man. That way some great people get opportunity for copulation."

That ignorant but young girl Mringānkdattā said that she wished for copulation, "O dear! My body is feeling sensation. It has become passionate to hear your story. Is there any way that a male can come here?"

It was the right moment for him. The cunning disciple of the cunning guru said, "If you wish like that then I tell you, O darling! I am blessed by Lord Vishnu that I can change into a man with my wish in nights. Then, now I am changing into a male for you."

He said that and took the pill out of his mouth and became Manahswāmi, the handsome young man. That night they enjoyed physical pleasure immensely. After that it became a daily affair. Manahswāmi remained a girl during the day and at night he would make love with the wife of the minister's son as a young man.

Now only a few days were left for the minister's son to return from the pilgrimage. He hatched a plan. The wife of minister's son too cooperated and they ran away.

This news came to Mooladeva. He was waiting for an opportunity. He again became the old Brahmin and went to king Yashahketu and requested, "O Emperor! I have searched out my son and brought with me. Now, please give me my daughter-in-law."

Out of the fear for curse the king discussed the matter with his minister and told the Brahmin, "O Brahmin! I don't know where your daughter-in-law gone. I ask for your forgiveness. For this crime, I'm giving my daughter to your son as a punishment to this crime."

Now, the cunning and fake Brahmin acted his part well, he showed anger, used rough language and made the king look ordinary. The king repeatedly requested him and gave his daughter, Shashiprabhā, to his fake son Shashi in marriage that was solemnized there.

In this way that Mooladeva returned with his son and newly wed daughter-in-law. Manahswāmi came to know of it. He returned and demanded his wife from Shashi as he had married her earlier according to the rule of Gandharvas. He said, "Give this Shashiprabhā to me. When she was unmarried I married her as Gandharvas do with the help of my Guru. But Shashi said, "O Fool! Who are you? What relation you have with her? What is the proof? She is my wife? Her father betrothed her to me in ritualistic marriage in the presence of Fire."

They both had made relation with that girl through cunningness. They fought but their fight did not resolve the matter. It was unclear as to who was the rightful husband of Shashiprabhā.

After finishing the story, Vetāla asked, "O Emperor! Keep my curse pronounced earlier in your mind and tell me who the rightful husband is? Whom should she be given?"

Vikram answered, "I feel that she is the lawful wife of Shashi because her father gave her to Shashi and kept Fire as witness according to religion and Scriptures. Manahswāmi had stealthily married her according to Gandharva tradition. A thief has no right on others' property that is stolen. "

Vetāla heard it and vanished from his shoulder, and went to the tree where he resided. Without getting bewildered from the supernatural and magical show of Vetāla, the king moved forward to take him to the Monk, that very night.

the detriment of another party. It can range from impersonation to other defects.

Modern management must take heed of and must be conscious

is impersonation, misrepresentation, fake identity, spurious

'Creative thinking brings a problem in view before it is created; and solves it before it gets an opportunity to play havoc.'

16

An executive looks for notions, intelligence and purpose,
He cannot work on emotions or intentions dubious,
In place of bowing down to passion he prefers rational ways:
Stimulates creativity in all and gets everything surplus.

King Yashodhar and Unmādini

King Vikram Sen reached the rosewood tree and picked up the human corpse and carried it on his shoulder and confidently walked towards the Buddha Monk. The Vetāla in the dead body started another story to King Vikram.

On the bank of River Ganges there was an ancient city of Kanakpur ruled by a powerful King named Yashodhar. King Yasodhar was known for his splendour, majesty and valour. It seemed as if the creator mixed the glow of both the sun and moon to create the bright halo behind his head. He was full of valour and benevolence.

In the Kingdom, there was a rich merchant who had a beautiful and sexy daughter Unmādini. Whosoever saw her got filled up with an intense desire for physical union with her. The merchant, knowing the ethics well went to king and said, "O divine king! I have a daughter of marriageable age and she is like the jewel of all the three worlds. I don't want to marry that girl to anyone else without first proposing her to you her. O Lord! You are entitled to take all the jewels of the world so please accept her in marriage and oblige me."

The King heard him patiently and sent a few Brahmins to make a report on the qualities of that girl. The Brahmins went were infatuated by her beauty and magical attraction. They came to the conclusion that if the King marries this girl, he would immediately forget the kingdom and get lost in her charm and the kingdom will go to ruins.

Finally they gave a false report to the king that the girl has the qualities that will ruin the kingdom. On the basis of the report, the king refused to marry the merchant's daughter. Then the merchant married off his daughter to Senāpati (the Chief Commander of the Army). She lived happily with her husband at his house.

Time passed. The beautiful spring season came. One day, King Yashodhar came out on an elephant to enjoy the festivities of *Basantotsava*. The King being so handsome, it was announced in advance that young married women should stay indoors as their glances might lead to infatuation for the king.

Unmādini heard the announcement and decided to defy it as she was insulted when the king refused to marry her. So, she deliberately went to the roof top and showed herself to the king. The king went mad to see that passionate beauty that he fainted.

The servants took him to the palace and he recovered. He enquired into the matter and came to know that it was Unmādini whose proposal he had rejected. He was angry with the Brahmins who had given a false report. As a punishment, he exiled them from his kingdom.

Now the King was completely absorbed in her memory. His heart, mind, memory, thought and meditation were absorbed in her image. Thinking like that he kept burning in the intense desire of lust. The effect was that he grew weaker day by day. On the one hand, it was immoral to lust for the wife of someone else that too for a king. So he kept this secret to himself despite persistent enquiry by his friends. But finally he divulged the secret cause of his pain and growing weakness to one of his closest pals.

The friends assured him "Don't worry. It's not difficult. She is under control. Why don't you copulate with her?" But that religious king refused to accept their suggestion.

Baldhar, the commander in Chief and the husband of Unmādini came to know of it. He was in pain. How can he see his master and the king dying for his wife? He went to the king and offered him his wife. When his Commander said that the king was angry. He outrightly rejected his prayer and said, "I'm the king. How can I do something irreligious? It is better to die than to indulge in sinful act."

Saying so, the king rejected the immoral offer because the men with sublime nature and character give their life but would not deviate from the path of religion and ethics.

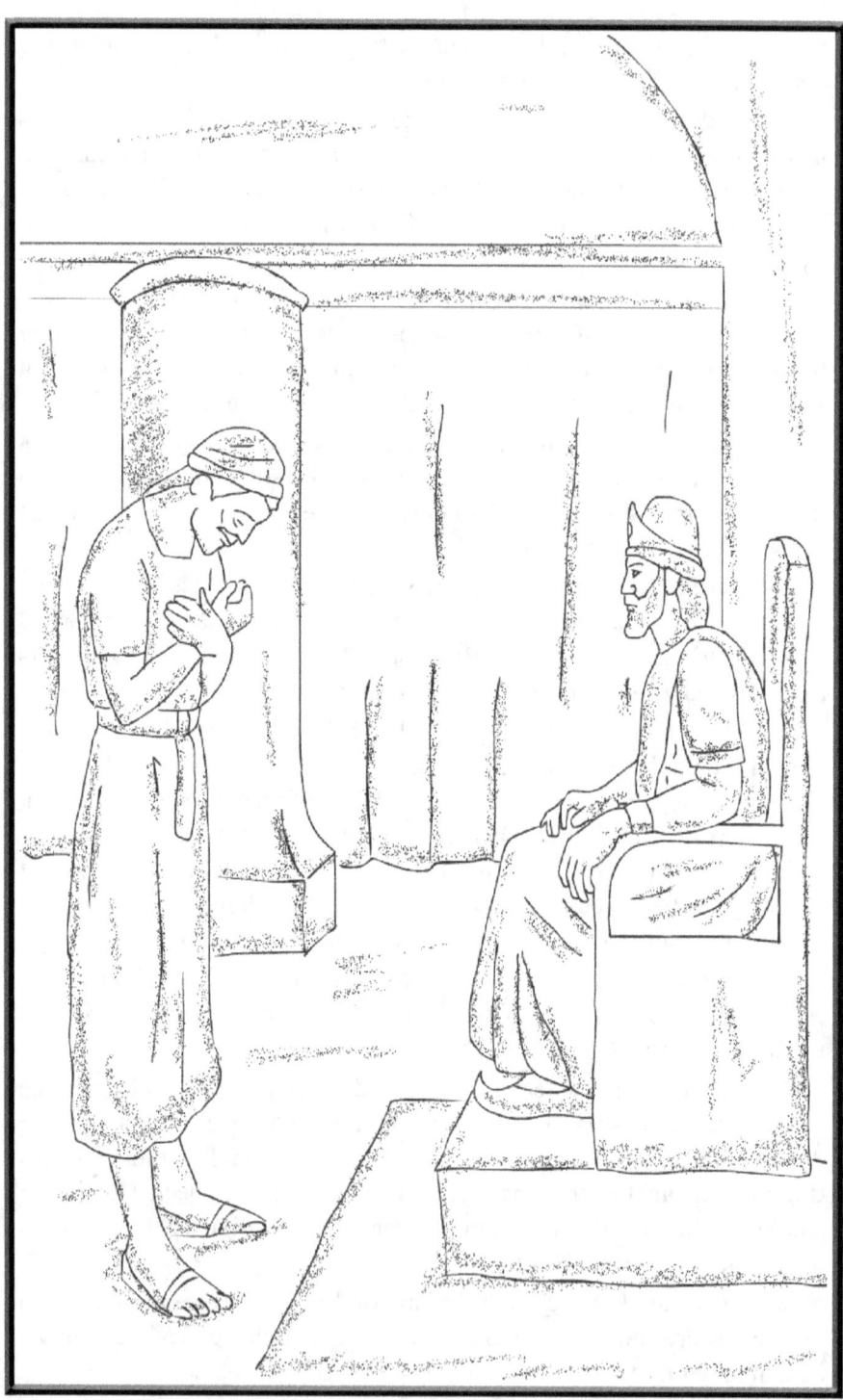

The King burnt inside in sexual desire for that extremely passionate woman; grew weaker and eventually died. The Commander too could not bear the pain of the death of the king. He entered the blazing fire and was gutted. It is difficult to know and describe the character of a devotee.

After finishing the story, Vetāla asked, "O Emperor! Who is greater: the king or the commander? You must answer with the previous curse in mind."

Vikram replied, "I treat the king to be superior."

Vetāla heard it and said satirically, "O Emperor! Why is that Commander not greater? He had copulated with that woman. He knew that pleasure. Yet he offered her to the king. Moreover, when the king died he sacrificed his own life. The king had rejected his wife without enjoying the pleasure of copulation."

The king heard Vetāla and laughingly answered him, "It is true but it's not so wonderful. It is the religious duty of the servants to save their master even at the cost of their own life. Kings are full of ego like elephants. They break the barriers of religion and indulge in physical pleasure. Wisdom and conscience flows out of them with the water of their ceremonious installation as the king. Although, this king Yoshodhar was undisputed king of the earth; passionately restless for the enchanting beauty of Unmādini; he preferred to die. He did not violate his religious dictates. That is why that valiant king is greater in my eyes."

Vetāla heard it and vanished from his shoulder, and went with his magical power to the tree where he resided. Without getting bewildered from the supernatural and magical show of Vetāla, the king moved forward to take him to the Monk, that very night.

de ciso

circumstance.

passion.

trend.

17

Every executive is entitled to individual approach,
Where he can leave enough space and yet encroach
With synchronized mind, idea, work and goal
With ever-flowing energy can praise or reproach.

Chandraswāmi

That night the burning *ghāta* was infested with wild carnivores that had come to eat the leftovers. It was a dreadful sight. The tongues looked like burning red flames and flames appeared to be red tongues. The sight was ghostly and ghosts were moving freely. That was a difficult night.

When Vikram reached his destination, the rosewood tree, he found many similar Vetālas hanging upside down by that tree. He could not decide which one was the real Vetāla. They were similar in appearance and were created by the magical prowess of Vetāla. Vikram said, "Oh! What is it? Is this illusory Vetāla wasting my time? Whom should I take out of these many Vetālas? I'm unable to know the original one. If I fail to take him to Buddha Monk and if the night passes out then I will enter fire. I would be a laughing stock."

The king thought loudly. Vetāla realised that Vikram was a man of strong principles. He was satisfied with the courage of the king. He took off the illusory creation. Now, there was only one human corpse left with Vetāla in it. So, the king put him up on his shoulder; and confidently and fearlessly, walked faster but silently towards the Buddha Monk.

The Vetāla in the dead body on the shoulders of King Vikram said, "O Emperor! If you are not bored with my stories then I'm telling you yet another one. Listen: There was a famous city called Ujjaini in the sequence

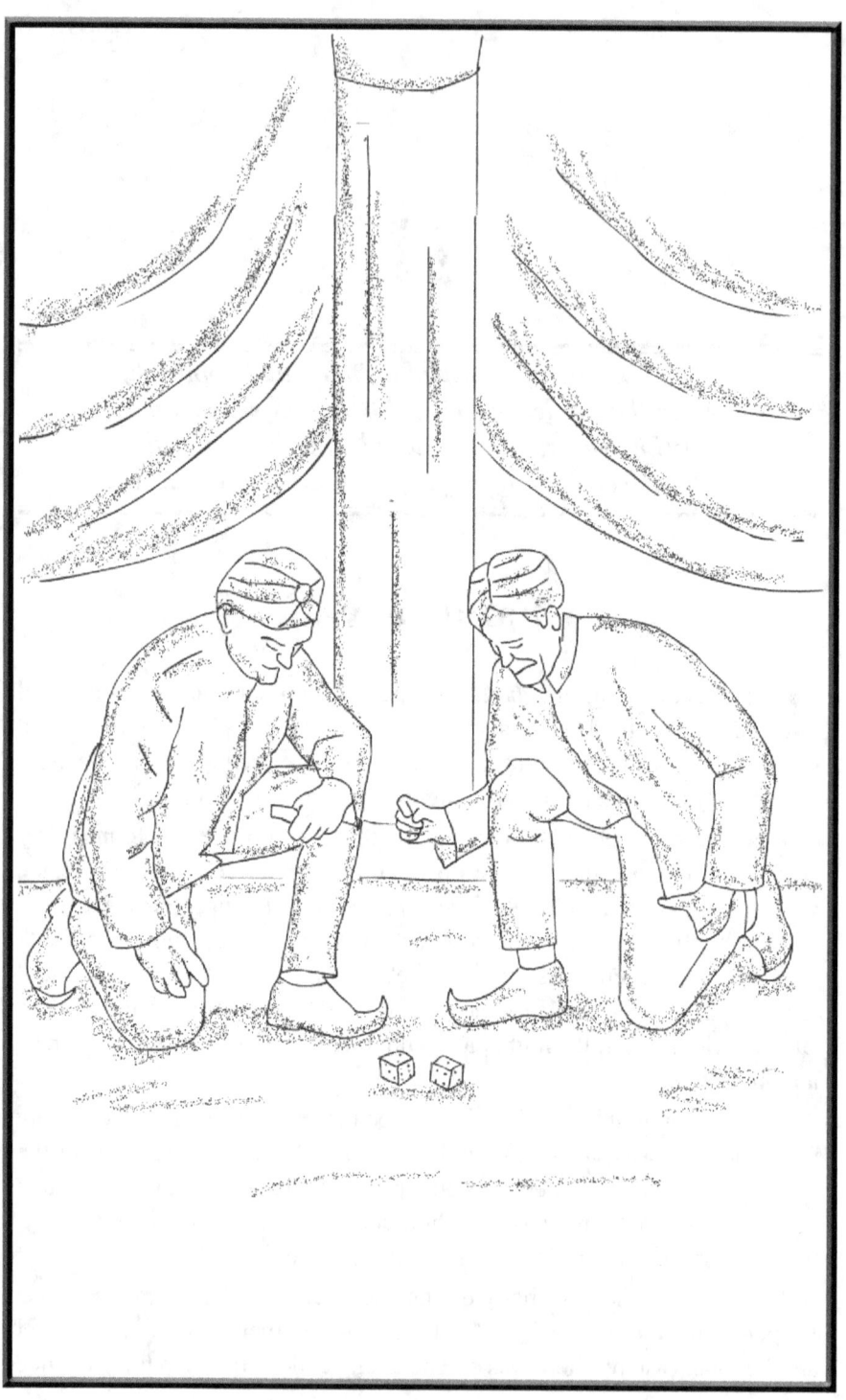

of Bhogawati and Amarāwati, created by Lord Shiva. He was pleased with the penance of Pārvati who was attracted towards him because of his achievements and special and strange qualities. These were created for her pleasure.

In Ujjaini, the people were religious and virtuous. There was cunningness in the moving eyebrows of young girls and there was no cunningness elsewhere. In the city there was darkness only during nights but there was no ignorance in men. There was satire as a figure of speech in the words of the poets but there was no ironical tone anywhere else. There was stillness and coldness in pearls, sandal and moon but it foolishness was not found at other places.

The city was ruled by a king named Chandraprabha who had a minister Devaswāmi – famous, religious, and virtuous. He knew most of the Scriptures and performed many *yagyas*. His son Chandraswāmi thought himself to be a great player of dice. He used to through it here and there and had practiced to throw it in his own way for desired results. He used to do it particularly with black dice. He boasted that he could win over the wealth of any rich person; even that of Alkāpati.

One day Chandraswami went to a gambling centre and started gambling against the cunning and professional men who had devised their technique of winning the wealth of the opponent. He started losing and before the close he lost everything including his clothes. He took loan on oral promise and lost that money too.

They asked for the return but he had no money to return. So, the proprietor of the center ordered him to be beaten black and blue. After being thrashed heavily his body grew hard and still like stone. He did not move for a few days from that place.

The cruel proprietor called his men and announced, "This man is almost dead. Take him out and throw in a well. I will pay his debt." The henchmen carried Chandraswāmi to a forest and were searching a well to throw him but they could not spot a well. An old and experienced cunning gambler, suggested them, "He is almost dead. What is the use of throwing him into a well? Leave him here. We can go back and say that he has been thrown into a well. They all accepted his suggestion; left him there and returned back.

When the cunning gamblers left the place, slowly Chandraswāmi rose up and entered a lonely temple of Lord Shiva. He regained his senses and thought, "Oh! It's painful. These cunning gamblers took me into confidence and robbed me. I'm almost naked and dusty. Where can I go in this pitiable condition? What will the father, brothers and relatives say to me? Then I will stay here till the evening then will go out during the night in search of some food."

Tired and naked he took rest there. Evening set in. At that time, a mendicant like Lord Shiva with ash smeared over the body with a trident in hand appeared and entered the temple. He saw Chandraswāmi and asked, "Who are you?" Then he narrated the events in short. He heard all and then said, "O young man! You have come to my hermitage! You are a hungry guest! Come on! Take bath! And share a part of the alms!"

But Chnadraswāmi refused saying, "O Mendicant! I'm a Brahmin, how can I eat a part of alms that you have begged?"

The mendicant took him to his hut and out of love for the guest he chanted the mantras that fulfilled all wishes. He had perfected that science in 24 years of rigorous penance. When he chanted the mantras a woman appeared and asked, "What should I do?"

He said, "Extend hospitality to this guest."

She said, "I will obey." The moment she said there appeared a beautiful garden along with a city of gold before Chandraswāmi. Beautiful dames came out and pleaded to Chandraswāmi, "O Handsome youth! Come on, take bath and your meal then enjoy my mistress."

She took him inside and gave him a fragrant bath and smeared fragrance on him; gave him nice clothes and then took him to another room. The young man found there another beautiful girl that was created by God just for the sake of fun. She rose up and welcomed him in traditional way. She shared the seat with him. He was given a variety of delicious food, and fruits to eat, and then betel to chew. They slept together and enjoyed the night.

In the morning, when he woke up, he saw only the Shiva Temple. There was neither the dreamy city with everything nor the divine lady with whom he had spent the night. He was restless. He hurried out. He saw that smiling mendicant. He asked about his experience during the night. He described it in short and concluded, "I did spend my night in pleasure but I would not survive without that divine beauty."

The mendicant laughed and said, "Wait here. During the night, you would get the same pleasure."

In this way, helped by that mendicant, Chandraswāmi enjoyed everything every night. Slowly he was impressed by the magical power of that mendicant. Then, one day he requested him, "If you are actually kind to me then I pray thee to teach me this science that has such wonderful effect."

He saw the eagerness and heard the request; then the Mendicant said, "O Young man! This science is beyond your control. It is perfected inside water. In order to deceive the person in penance it spreads such illusions that the devotee in meditation fails. He sees his complete previous life from birth to youth and from there to departure, before and after marriage and with son; then he feels that he is my friend and that one is my enemy and the feelings of love, hate and revenge engulf him; and in such a way that the devotee fails. That person remembers neither this science nor the purpose what and why was he chanting or was for penance.

The one who is successful, meditates, chants the *Mantra* inside the water for a long period and knows that all the attractions so shown, were magical and illusory. With full knowledge of this fact he enters fire. Only he comes out of water and envisions the right science. Only able disciples get and perfect this science. If it is given to a weak disciple, then the preceptor loses its knowledge and command over it. With my perfection you are getting everything; then there is no need for such requests. The available divine material and woman that you are getting and enjoying will come to an end only when I lose this science."

But Chandrasāmi was headstrong and rigid. He repeated his request with promises, "I'll be able to do everything, O Mendicant! Don't worry about it." Then that recluse promised to teach him that science and accepted him as his disciple.

The Mendicant brought him to the bank of the river and instructed, "My Child! While chanting the Mantras when you see the illusory world, then the science will bring you to regain senses and keep you conscious. Then you must enter the flamed fire. I will be here at the bank of the river waiting for you."

Saying so, he purged himself and the purification of Chandraswāmi was completed; and then he gave the Mantra to Chandraswāmi. The preceptor remained at the shore and the disciple entered the river with a force. He started chanting the Mantra inside water. Suddenly, he was overtaken by the illusion. He forgot this life and the act that he was performing. In that illusory world he took birth as the son of a Brahmin. He grew up. Sacred thread ceremony was arranged, completed his studies, got married and then became the father of many children while passing through the changing phases of pleasure and pain. Then he lived with his wife and children; and the parents and relatives for sometime.

In this way, he experienced false pleasures and pains of another life. Then, the preceptor chanted the Mantras that were capable of making and keeping him conscious. Chandraswāmi was immediately struck by its effect and regained his consciousness. He remembered his guru, he remembered his purpose and now, he realized that he has to enter the enflamed fire. When he was about to step on to the fire, the parents, wife, children and relatives surrounded him. They tried to stop him from self-immolation.

Though the emotional pressure was high and he had enjoyed a divine life, he wanted that science, so he went to the pyre ready at the bank of the river. There he again saw his old parents, weeping wife and children and grew weak in their love. He started thinking, "Ah! It is painful that they will vanish when I enter the fire. Will the words of the preceptor come true? I don't know it. Should I enter the fire? Or should I return to my house? How can the words of that great guru be false? I'll definitely enter the fire."

Thinking so, Chandraswāmi entered fire. The fire was cold like ice. He was full of wonder. He shook off the fear of fire and came out of the river. He found his guru seated at the bank on the sand. He prostrated on the feet of the guru. The guru asked about his experiences and he narrated everything up to the entry into fire that was cold and how he came out of the river.

The guru said, "It seems, my child you have committed some mistake somewhere, otherwise, how the fire can change into ice for you. It is the most difficult part in perfecting this science."

Having found the guru worried, Chandraswāmi said, "O guru! I don't remember that I have made any mistake anywhere."

In order to test it the guru tried to recite the mantra but he had forgotten it. He could not recall the mantras. He asked his disciple to repeat it but the disciple too had lost the mantra. They were aggrieved at the loss of the rare science. They left that place.

After finishing the story, Vetāla asked, "O Emperor! Please clarify my doubt. Although, every instruction was followed correctly yet why the science was lost?"

King Vikram answered, "O the master of Yoga! I feel in this way you are deliberately wasting my time. Yet, I tell you the reason. A man cannot get success and perfection only by doing some difficult work. Perfection is achieved through purity; with purity of intention and purity of deeds.

The mind of that ignorant Brahmin youth was enlightened by the guru yet it raised doubts; and failed to get perfection in that science. On the other hand, the guru lost that science as he had given it to unworthy disciple."

Vetāla heard it and vanished from his shoulder, and went to the tree where he resided. Without getting bewildered from the supernatural and magical show of Vetāla, the king decided to take him to the Monk, that very night. The King almost ran after him.

Importance of Training

maintained by the trainee. Trainees are young managers or future directors. They must not be indifferent rather they need to be impatient for success

operate.

pastime, an entertainment. In most of the other countries it has

fake industries to manufacture arms or spurious medicines and

or crime. The faster, such money comes, the faster it goes.

projects and better opportunities and better options for business and gain.

instruments and machinery.

morning.

'A proper image of a company must be created and maintained in public mind.'

18

An executive faces often tricky situations and relationships,
When he can neither run away nor save neck nor use whip,
He finds himself in a perfect dilemma of strange nature:
Ghostly demands of employees; or sinking organization's ship

King Suryaprabha and Prince Chandraprabha

To take the tricky Vetāla, King Vikram reached the rosewood tree again and picked up the human corpse, put it on his shoulder and walked silently but hastily towards the Buddha Monk. The Vetāla in the dead body said, "O Emperor! This time I'll tell you a very interesting story. Now listen."

There was a heavenly city called Vakralaka where King Suryaprabha ruled. The King was very benign in providing all welfare and facilities to the people. He obliterated all enemies. The king had all prosperity and possessed everything needed but he was sad because he had no children, though, he had many queens.

At that time in the Tāmralipti city there was a leading businessman called Dhanapala who had enormous wealth. A nymph from the heaven, due to a curse, took birth as his daughter. When she grew young that merchant died. The relatives usurped all his wealth. His wife Hiranyawati took her daughter Dhanawati along with the gold and jewels and kept them secretly somewhere fearing harm from the relatives. Moving in the pitch darkness Hiranyawati hit the shoulders of a thief who was hanging on a sharp cross. The thief said, "The hard push of your shoulder gave me lot of pain. Who smeared salt on my wounds?"

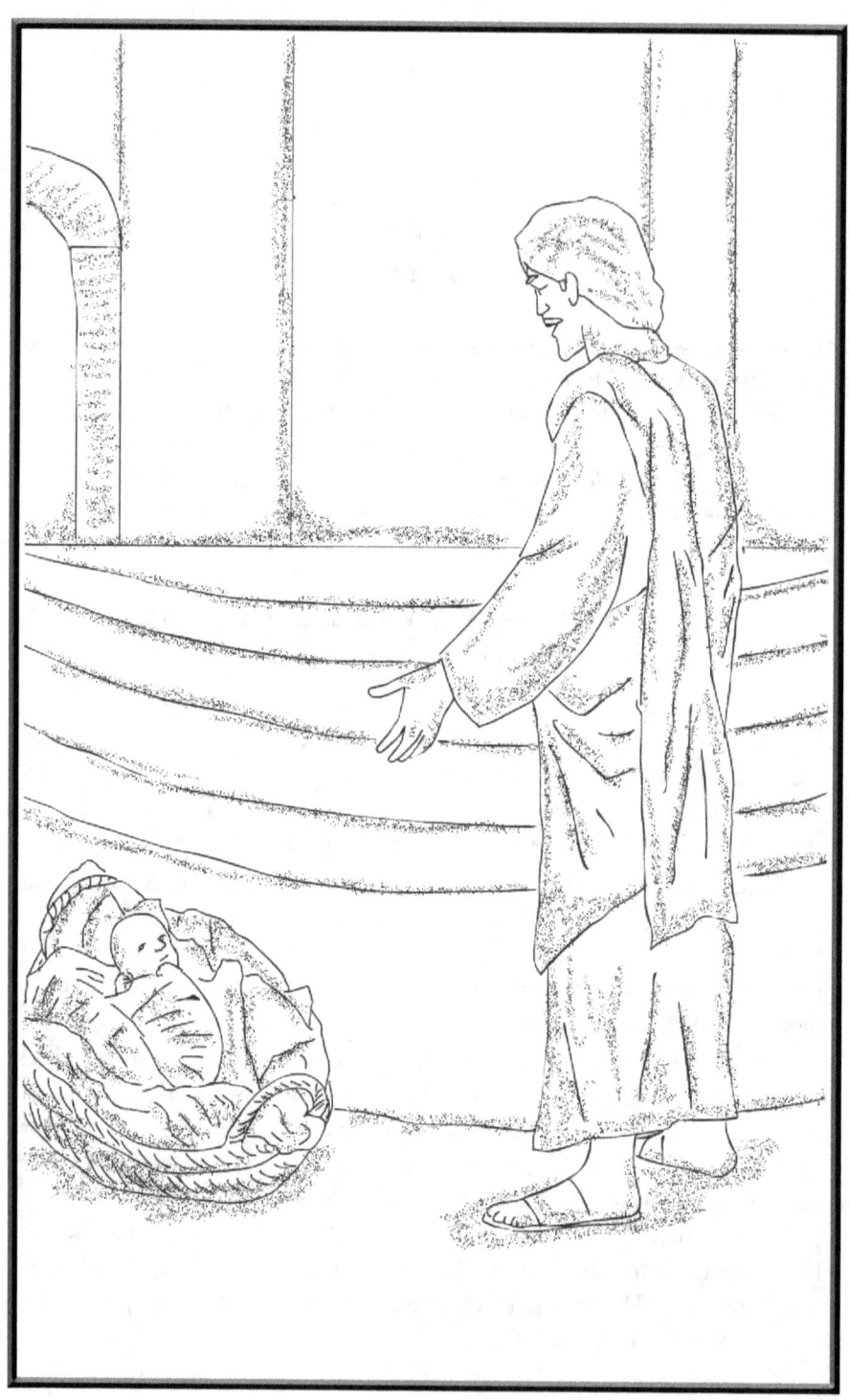

The wife of the merchant asked, "Who are you?" She was trembling with fear. The thief answered, "I'm a thief who has been hanged this way. I'm on the cross yet I'm not dying for I'm a great sinner. Whatever may happen, O Lady, tell me who are you and where are you going in this deep darkness?"

The merchant's wife narrated her story. In the meantime the Sun god lighted the face of east. When there was adequate light the thief watched the daughter closely and said to her mother, "O Lady! Listen to my prayer! I will give you one thousand gold coins. Please give your daughter to me". She laughed, "What will you gain from her when you are about to die?"

The thief said again, "I have no age left, and I have no son. As I have no son I can't get to heaven. With my order she would conceive from any person and give birth to a son. He will be the son of my legacy. This is what I would request her. Then, O mother! Please grant my desire."

Lusting for wealth, merchant's wife accepted the offer. She sprinkled some water and announced her decision, "I offer my daughter to you". Then, the thief too repeated his orders to Dhanwati, the daughter of the merchant, and permitted her to conceive a son from any person she liked. But that child would be known as his son. After giving the orders, the thief said, "O mother! Go to that banyan tree and dig up near its root. I have secretly kept one thousand gold coins there. Take that wealth. After my death put my dead body into fire and immerse the bones at some holy place. When you have done it go to a city called Vakrolaka. Thanks to King Suryaprabha there is strong administration and you will face no disturbance or oppression. So you can live safely and peacefully there."

The thief felt thirsty and drank the water given by the lady and he died immediately. Then the merchant's wife dug up the place and excavated the gold and went to the house of one of her husband's friends. With his assistance she cremated the thief's dead body; collected the bones and immersed them at a river near a pilgrimage centre.

The merchant's wife then secretly moved with a lot of wealth and reached the city Vakrolaka as suggested by the thief. There she bought the house of a merchant named Basudatta and started living in peace along with daughter Dhanawati. During that period, a teacher named Vishnuswāmi lived there who had a handsome disciple named Manahswāmi. Though he belonged to a high family, he had unlimited sexual passion and used to go to a prostitute, Hansāwali. Paying her five hundred gold coins he would enjoy a night of physical pleasures. But it was difficult to arrange that kind of wealth every now and then. So he went into depression and became weaker and weaker every day.

One day, Dhanwati was sitting on the roof and she saw Manahswāmi. Though he was weak, she was attracted by his handsome figure. She recalled the order of her thief-husband to seduce any man for a son. Her mother realised that Dhanwati was attracted towards the young man. They sent a maid to call that young man. That morally corrupt young Brahmin replied, "If you can pay me five hundred gold coins for my meeting with Hansāwali, I can spend a night with Dhanwati."

As demanded, Dhanwati sent five hundred gold coins to him and Manahswāmi arrived at her residence to provide his 'service'. He was delighted to see that extremely beautiful girl. He spent that night enjoying her and left the place early in the morning. Soon, Dhanwati conceived a child. After nine months, she gave birth to a healthy son who was endowed with all attributes of a royal child. But the mother and the daughter had reasons to worry. During the night Lord Shiva appeared in their dreams and ordered, "Along with one thousand gold coins leave this child at the gate of King Suryaprabha on the scaffold."

As they had firm faith in Lord Shiva they obeyed His order and left the child on the scaffold as suggested along with the gold coins.

At the same time, Lord Shiva appeared in the dream of King Suryaprabha and ordered, "O king awake! There is a child, with all royal regalia on the scaffold at the gate. Someone has abandoned the child. Accept him immediately."

In the morning, the king came out with the guards and found the child on the scaffold along with the gold coins as described in the dream. He saw the signs of flag and royal umbrella on the hands and feet of the child. The child was handsome and attractive. He announced, "Lord Shiva has gifted this worthy son." Saying so, he lifted the child in both his hands and entered the queenly abode. On the twelfth day he arranged a great festival and named the son "Chandraprabha".

Time passed. The prince Chandraprabha grew into a handsome, kind, compassionate and benevolent young man. King Suryaprabha found his son to be worthy of holding a kingdom intact and ruling well. As per religious rituals he made him the king and himself left for Varanasi. The king Chandraprabha ruled very well even as Suryaprabha went for hard penance. But Suryaprabha could not endure the hardships of penance and died. The religious king Chandraprabha completed the last rites in a befitting way as per the Scriptures. Then, one day he called all the ministers and announced, "I can't be free from the debt of my father. I'll immerse his remains in the scared river Ganges. After that I shall proceed to Gayā for the last ritualistic offerings. So, I'll proceed on a pilgrimage."

The ministers dissuaded the king, "It's not correct to do it because a kingdom is a storehouse of disturbances. The life of a traveller is full of dangers while a king is safe and secure in his kingdom."

The King replied, "It is useless to be pessimistic. I have to go on pilgrimage for my father. I will visit as many centres of pilgrimage as possible. The body is perishable. No one knows what will happen next. In my absence you all will look after the kingdom."

On the auspicious day, the King departed with Brahmins and priests. The King was pleased to see different types of people, natural sights and colourful clothing. He performed the last rites and again boarded his chariot and reached Prayāga, where the three rivers: Gangā; Yamunā and Saraswati meet. He observed fasting; gave a lot in charity then came to Kāshi, the declared abode of Lord Shiva. There too he observed fasting for three days, performed Poojā of Lord Shiva and then started his journey towards Gayā.

After crossing over different mountains, rivers and cities he at last reached Gayā. All the religious rituals were performed; adequate offerings made to Brahmins and charity done to the poor. When he offered the rice-ball as offering to his father three different looking hands appeared to accept it.

The King was astonished to see it. "What is this? Why three hands? In which hand should I place the offering?" He enquired with the Brahmin. They explained the matter, "O Emperor! One is definitely the hand of a thief as it has an iron rod for breaking the walls. The second one is the hand of a Brahmin as it has 'pious ritualistic thread in his wrist'. The third one is the hand of a king. It has royal signs and wearing a big and priceless ring. But we don't know in whose palm should this rice-ball be placed? What is it?" The king heard the explanation but he was unable to decide what to do.

After finishing the story, Vetāla asked, "O Emperor! Whom should that *pinda* (the offering of rice-ball) be given? Please clarify it. And, also keep in mind the curse given earlier."

Vikram answered, "Vetāla! As King Chandraprabha is the one who brought him up, not the other two; he should be given the offering. Although, the Brahmin is his biological father, ethically the King is not his son because he had sold himself for a few gold coins to spend that night of physical union. The King would have been king Suryaprabha's foster son, had he not received the gold coins placed on the scaffold. King Suryaprabha raised the child with that money. Actually, her mother was ordered to bear a son from any male; the merchant's wife and daughter too were paid for their services; the young Brahmin's semen too was bought with that money; and he was fostered up with that money. So he is the real son of the thief. That is why the offering should be placed in his hand for his salvation. It is my opinion."

Vetāla heard it and vanished from his shoulder, and went to the tree where he resided. King Vikram followed the Vetāla to take him to the Monk.

Strong Administration: This is the key to management. Apart

'A deviation from an established and agreed path brings the ruin faster. Very hard labour and great sacrifi ce is needed to change the disastrous trend.'

19

Fear does not come from outside, it's generated inside;
It devours strength, energy, will and breaks open wide;
If not shaken off in time, it captures mental faculty, and
From there towards inhumanity begins unstoppable slide.

King Chandrāloka and A Seer's Daughter

After that, slowly and surely that king Vikram Sen reached that rosewood tree and picked up the human corpse with laughing Vetāla in it, put it up on his shoulder walked faster but silently towards the Buddha Monk.

The Vetāla said, "O Emperor! You don't realize what you are doing. But you are confident and headstrong. Go back and enjoy the pleasures of night. It's not good for you to carry me to that despicable mendicant. If you yet insist on doing it then I tell you this story."

There was a city named Chitrakuta. It was ruled by a king named Chandrāloka who was a precious jewel among the kings; and is the one who makes nectar flow from the eyes of the beggars and the lovers. The scholars called him to be the pillar to tie up the elephant; the birthplace of charity and the luxurious place of beauty. He had everything but he lacked a wife worthy of him.

Once, the King in order to control his restlessness went on a hunting expedition accompanied by soldiers on horse-back. He excited the horse to run faster and crossed over to another forest covering a long distance in a short time. Unfortunately, the King lost his way and direction. He saw a

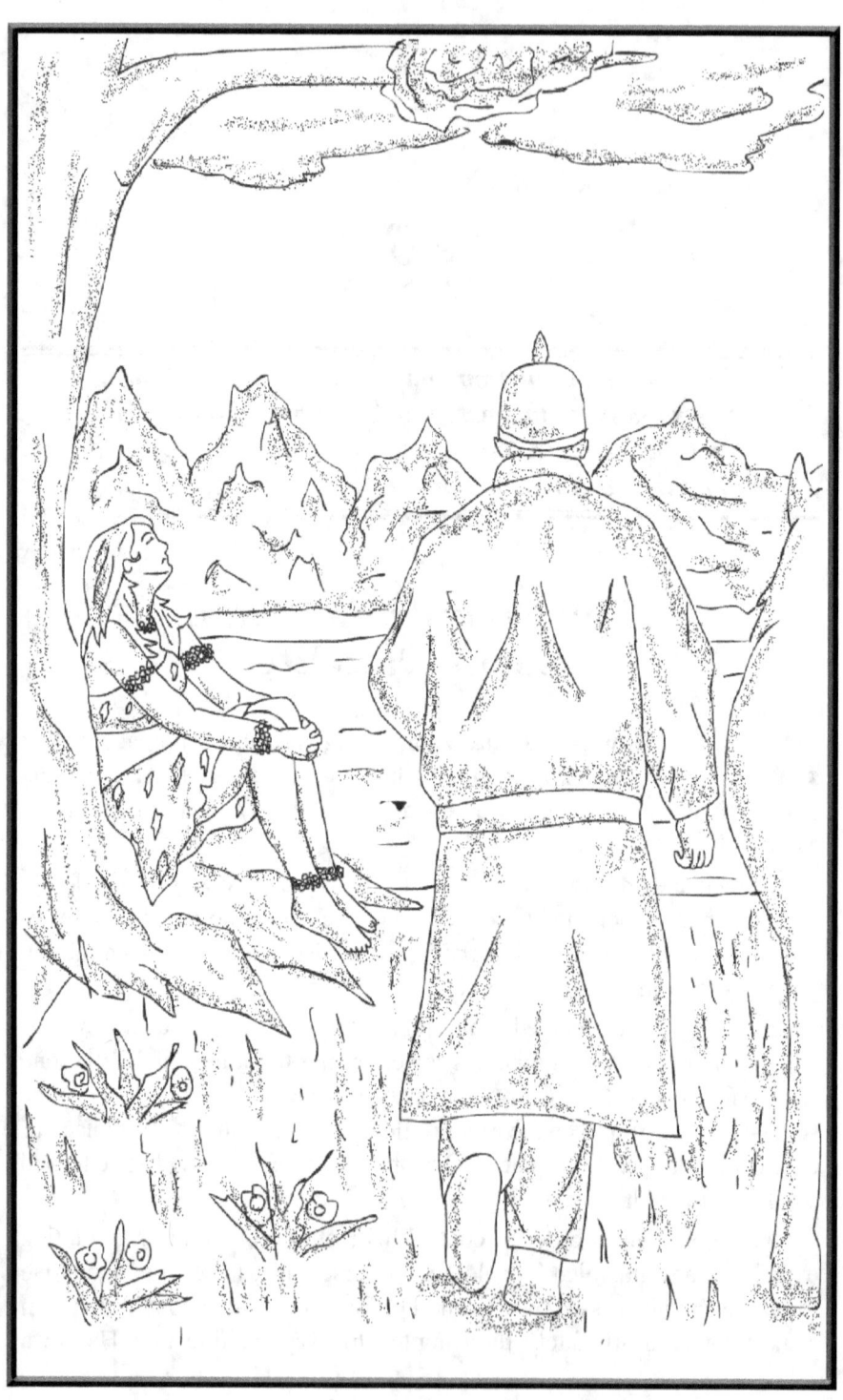

beautiful pond. He took the saddle off the horse, gave it water and a bath, then fed grass and brought it under the shade of a tree.

The King also took a bath and refreshed himself. Suddenly his eyes fell on an Ashoka tree under which a girl was wearing the ornaments of flowers; had tiger skin as her cloth; had a high plait on head. She seemed to be the daughter of some sage; she was wonderfully beautiful. The desire for lust overpowered the King. He thought, "Who can be this dame? Is she Sāvitri who had come to take bath in the pond? Or is she Pārvati herself who has gone into penance again because of fresh separation from her husband? I must go to her to know her identity."

Slowly the King went to the dame. She too saw him coming towards her. She stopped making garland of flowers. She kept on staring at him as she was attracted towards him. She thought, "Who is this handsome man in this forest? Is he a Vidyādhar (a Genie)? The desires of my eyes are fulfilled."

One of her friends answered the King's query, "O Gentleman! The great dancer of Indra gave birth to this daughter of Maharishi Kanva. She grew up in the hermitage. She is called Indiwarprabhā. It was on the order of her father that she came to this pond to take a bath. The hermitage of her father is nearby to this place."

The King mounted the horse and rode up to the hermitage of the Rishi to ask for the hand of his daughter. Having entered the hermitage the king saw Maharishi Kanva who was surrounded by trees-like mendicants; his glow was that of the Moon. He touched his feet. The Rishi extended all hospitality to the king. When the king had taken rest then the Rishi said to the king, "O My child Chandrāloka! I say that is beneficial to you. I know how the living beings live in fear. Then why do you kill these deer and other animals without any specific purpose? The God created weapons so that the Kshatriyas can protect the weaker ones. Protect the people as the religion says. Wipe out the bad elements. With the help of horses and elephants try to control wealth that moves very fast; enjoy the kingship, be benevolent and offer charity, spread fame to different directions. This hunting is helping the god of death. Stop hunting forever. What is the use of this dangerous game? Have you not heard the story of King Pāndu?"

The King knew his duties but had fallen prey to restless emotions. He praised the Rishi, "O Great man! You have opened my eyes. I'm very much obliged to you. From today onwards I will quit hunting. Now, all living beings live happily without fear."

The Rishi said, "I am happy at your decision to protect the living beings, so, you can ask for a boon."

The king thought that it is the right time to express the wish. He said, "O Great man! If you are really pleased with me then give me your daughter Indiwarprabhā."

His daughter, born out of a heavenly nymph, had just returned after taking bath. He gave her to the king in marriage. The marriage was solemnized. All those that lived in the hermitage came up to the boundary of the hermitage to bid her farewell. The king took Indiwarprabhā upon his horse and returned to his kingdom.

The sun set behind the peaks of the mountain. The king saw a peepal (banyan) tree at the bank of a pond that had long green branches and had a soft bed of green grass under it. The king decided to spend the night there.

He came down from the horse along with his beloved wife. He drank water from the pond and took rest with Indiwarprabhā. The moon came out taking off the clothes from darkness and started kissing the lips of east. Out of severe passion the king embraced Indiwarprabhā. They spent the night like serpents in love.

In the morning, as the king was ready to depart an extremely angry demon (Brahma-rākshas) with yellowish hair confronted him. He was ferocious in looks. Showing fire like anger from the eyes, he roared chiding the king, "O Sinner! Take me for Jwālāmukh (Volcanic) demon. This banyan tree is my abode. Even the gods don't insult it. You and your mistress by having sex under it, insulted me. Then take the punishment for your arrogance. O Licentious fellow! You are blinded by sexual pleasure. I will tear away your heart and drink your blood."

The king was sure he would not be able to kill the demon. Scared he looked towards his wife. She too was afraid of him. The king said humbly, "Unknowingly I may have committed a crime. Please forgive me. I'm a guest at your hermitage and have taken shelter here. I'll offer thee your desired man or animal for food, whichever you prefer. So, be please and check your anger."

The Brahmarākshas was pacified. He thought, 'It's all right. There is no harm in it.' He said, "O Emperor! If a very courageous, wise, learned, 7-year-old son of a Brahmin willingly gives himself on your behalf and if at the time of killing their parent hold his hands and legs tightly to the ground, then I'll leave you. But you have to give such a boy within seven days otherwise, there is no excuse for you and I would destroy your whole family."

The king accepted it out of fear. The Brahmarākshas instantly disappeared. The king thought, "Ah! I have fallen prey to hunting and sex and have been destroyed just like king Pāndu. Then, now I go to my own capital city and wait for the ultimate destiny to show itself."

Thinking thus, he returned to his city. He spent the rest of the day in pain and anguish although the people arranged a befitting function and celebrations to welcome the queen. The next day, he secretly told his ministers to find the youngster for a sacrifice. A wise minister suggested, "O Emperor! Don't worry. I will search out and bring such a gift as this earth is wonderful. You can get anything that you desire."

The minister so consoled the king, and got an idol of a seven year old child made of pure gold. Along with that gold idol the messengers of the king moved all around beating drum and making announcement like this, "This idol of gold decorated with jewels and one hundred villages will be given to such a seven year old son of a Brahmin who will willingly offer himself as a gift to the Brahmarākshas as food and at the time of killing the mother and father should hold the hands and legs of the boy to the earth."

There was a seven year old Brahmin boy in a village who has patience and was extremely handsome. From his childhood he had performed benevolent deeds and was an emblem of virtues. He heard the announcement and said to the announcer. "O gentleman! I'll give myself to you. Just wait. I'll explain it to my parents and return soon."

He said so and took their permission then went back to his parents. He said there, "O Mother! O father! I give this mortal body for the sake of all other living beings. Grant me permission for it. I take my idol made up of gold along with one hundred villages given by the king. This will free me from your debt and establish my benevolence. You would be rich forever and get many more sons."

The parents heard it and immediately raised objections, "O Son! What are you telling? Are you suffering from any disease? Or have the planets gone wrong? Otherwise, how can you talk in such a meaningless way? Who will allow his son to be killed only for money? Who will give his own body and life?"

The boy heard his parents and replied, "I have not gone mad. It's very important and meaningful. This body will die soon. It has innumerous impurities that should not be named. It is hateful and abode of pain. So, if some virtuous deeds are performed with it then it will become useful. This is the essence of life. The wise men say like that. And if the body is used to serve the parents then what else can be greater than that."

By saying so, the patient and determined child remained undeterred and forced his parents to accept his proposal. He returned and collected the idol of gold and related papers of hundred villages and gave it to his parents.

After finishing all such obligations he went towards Chitrakut with his parents led by the men of the king. The king was pleased to see that tender boy that had pure glow, and was a shield that protected the king and his family. Sandal was smeared over him and he was garlanded, then, brought to the Brahmarākshas on the back of an elephant. The priests drew circular lines under the banyan tree and performed rituals. When it was the time for offering, the dreadful Brahmarākshas, Jwālāmukha, appeared. He was chanting Veda mantras; walking here and there; taking wine of blood; his eyes glowing like fire; and darkening the directions with the brightness of his body.

The king saw him and said humbly, "O Spirit! This gift of human being has been brought for you. It's the seventh day of your oath. Please accept this gift in proper way."

When the king prayed like this, the Brahmarākshas licked the corners of his lips, and saw the valiant child that was lying as a gift. At that time, the great courageous and unshaken son of the Brahmin thought, "Whatever virtue I have earned with the gift of this body, even if I don't attain heaven or salvation, I must get the body again." The boy thought like that and the sky was filled with the Vimānas (planes) that showered flowers over him.

The boy was placed before the Brahmarākshas. His parents tightly caught his hands and legs; pushed hard towards the ground. When the king got ready with the open sharp sword then, the boy laughed. All the persons present there including the Brahmarākshas, abandoned their work and started looking at the boy. They stood motionless with heads bowed low in humility.

After finishing this strange story, Vetāla asked, "O Emperor! What was the reason that the boy started laughing when his end was near? I'm really very curious to know it. If you knowingly don't answer it then your head will break into hundred pieces."

King Vikram answered, "Now listen to the reason behind the laugh of the boy. Those who are weak and under threat must be saved by the parents; if the parents are not there then the king should save them. The Creator made them for that only. When they are not there then, he calls and requests, gods. One of them gives him shelter and protects him. But in the case of this child each one went against him. For the lust of money the parents caught the hands and feet; for his own protection the king was ready to cut him; and despite the fact that the Brahmarākshas is a spirit, he too came there to eat him. The fools are getting so degenerated for the mortal body that has a sad end and is the cause of anxiety and pain. It is a wonderful thing to make one's body immortal when Brahmā, Vishnu and Mahesh are definitely mortal. He felt deeply about their strange looking hallucination; and felt satisfied that his purpose is being solved; the boy was filled up with wonder and pleasure. That is why he laughed."

Vetāla heard it and vanished from his shoulder, and went to the tree where he resided. Without getting bewildered from the supernatural and magical show of Vetāla, the King decided to take him to the Monk, that very night.

Management.

management.

Terrorist or demonic attacks can be countered, not with weapons but with inner strength of moral character. Humanity is more powerful than the power of all human beings combined together.'

20

Self-exploration is the fairest of an executive's all,
A popular, fabulous, essential and an exciting call,
Smoothly feminine in appearance, strongly masculine in effect:
It's a practical pursuit that allows no failure and no fall.

The Story of Anangmanjari

King Vikram Sen reached that rosewood tree and picked up the human corpse with laughing Vetāla in it, put it up on his shoulder; and confidently walked faster towards the Buddha Monk.

The Vetāla on the shoulders of King Vikram said, "O Emperor! For freshness from fatigue, now listen to a story that contains ecstatic passion." For persons fallen from heaven there was another heaven like city called Vishālā. It was ruled by a strong king named Padmanābha. During his reign there was a great merchant who had the capacity to conquer Kuber, the Lord of Wealth in terms of his power of wealth.

The merchant had a daughter Anangmanjari. Through her, the Creator showed the image of a nymph. The merchant gave his daughter in marriage to another merchant Mani Vermā who lived in the famous city Tāmralipti. Being his only daughter, out of immense love the merchant could not separate from the daughter and hence he did not send her to her husband's house.

Mani Vermā was bitter but wife was dear to him. Once, very eager to meet his parents, Mani Vermā went to Tāmralipti. As summer came; his return journey was obstructed by hurdles like heat and fatigue experienced on the road.

One day, Anangmanjari, in nice make up and revealing clothes with sandal smeared body came and sat at the window of her room. She saw a handsome young man Kamlākar, the son of the royal priest who looked like a new god of love that had come out in search of Rati (the wife of Cupid) along with a faithful friend. He also saw her sitting up like a moon and was excited to see that incomparable beauty.

Having seen her Kamalākar's desire for lust grew. Somehow his friend brought him back to the house. Anangmanjari was equally affected by the desire for his companionship. She returned to her living room with her friend; but passion for lust lingered in her. She could only think about him as she lay lazily on her smooth and luxurious bed.

A few days passed. She felt ashamed about her passion and grew thin because of the pain of separation and looked jaundiced. She lost hope of meeting up with her lover.

One night she became so depressed that at night she came out of her room and went to the pond in the garden in order to commit suicide. She went to the family Goddess Durgā, whose idol was consecrated by her father, worshipped her and requested her, "O Goddess! I did not get Kamalākar as my husband in this life; then please unite me with him in my next life."

Praying so, just opposite the idol of the Goddess, she went to the Ashoka tree; and prepared a knot with her long scarf and got ready to hang herself. In the meantime, her friend woke up. Not finding her friend on the bed, she started searching and saw her trying to commit suicide. She cried, "Don't do it! Don't do it!"

The friend raced towards her and immediately untied the knot. She saw her friend and could not control her. She fell on the ground. Her friend consoled her and asked the reason behind the extreme step. She said, "O dear friend, Mālati! I'm under the bondage of my father and hence, unable to get my lover. So, I have no option other than dying. There is no pleasure in my life." She said this with pain and fainted."

Mālati thought, "She is very aggrieved. The orders of the god of love, has to be followed. She has fallen so low and in such a condition." Thinking thus, Mālati treated her with cold water and fresh air. She tried to bring her back to her normal self; prepared a bed of lotus leaves to cool her body and passion; and placed ice-cool garland of pearls in her neck.

Anangmanjari regained her senses and told her aide: "Dear friend! The garlands of pearls will not cool me down. If you want to see me alive then somehow make my lover meet me."

Mālati was kind and full of compassion, "The night has almost passed. Early in the morning I will bring your lover to you. So, have patience and

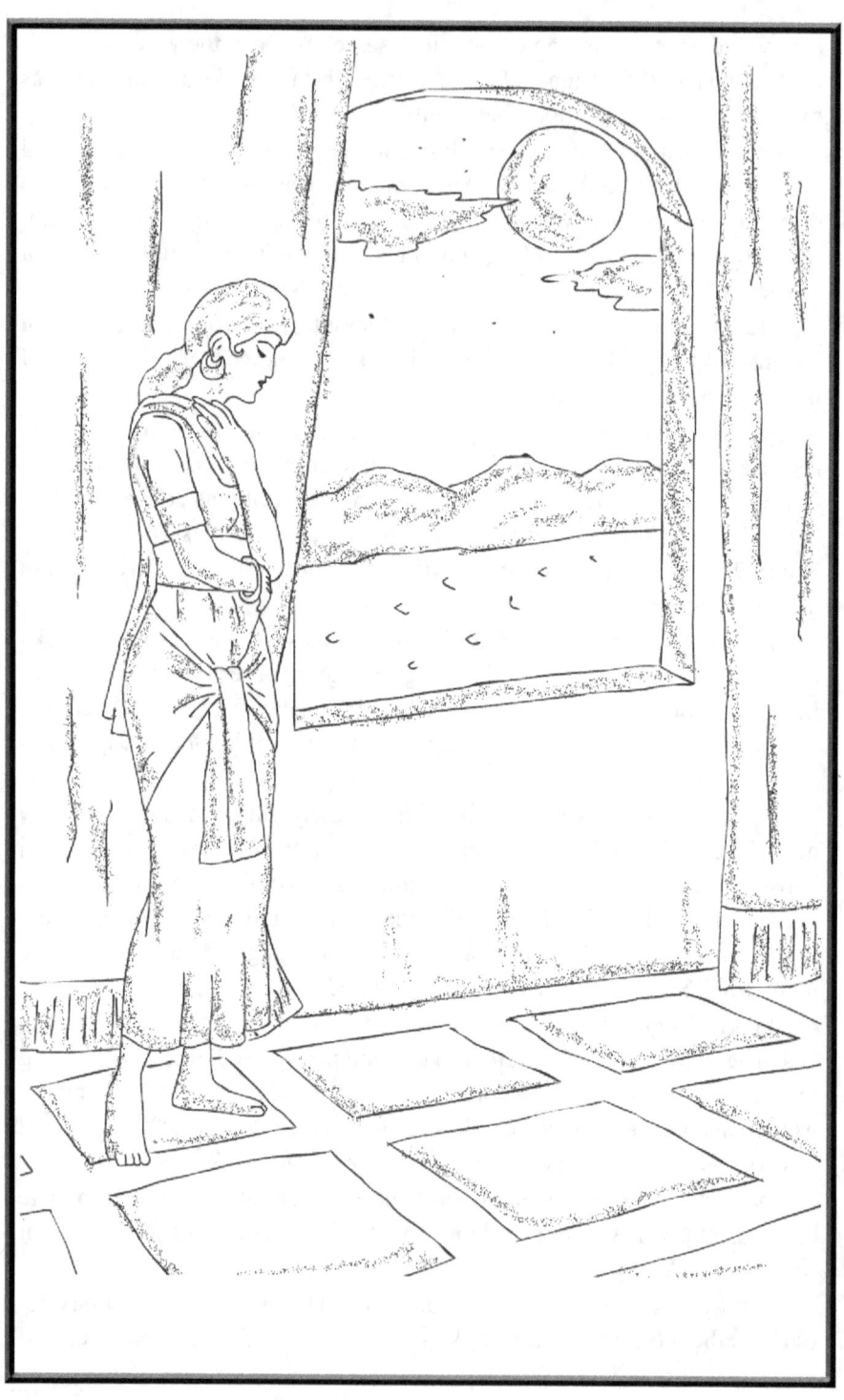

return to your bed." Anangmanjari was pleased. She gave a garland of pearls as reward to Mālati.

"Let us return now. You'll go in the morning to complete the task." They returned. In the morning, Mālati secretly searched out the house of Kamlākar and went there. She found him aggrieved and full of passion for Anangmanjari. He was lying on a bed of lotus leaves. His close friend was fanning him with a banana-leaf. He was burning in the fire of love. In order to be sure whether he too is in love with her friend or not Mālati, heard out their talk. Kamlākar's friend said, "Dear friend! For the time being, look at the beautiful garden around you and try to get lost in it. Don't be so excited."

Kamlākar responded, "My heart has been taken away by Anangmanjari. So, my heart is not in my body. How can I enlighten it. The god of love has changed me into a heartless quiver of arrows. So, please do something so that I can get the girl who has stolen my heart."

Having heard him and assured of his love for her friend, Mālati came out of the hiding place. She went to them and said, "O Handsome! Anangmanjari sent me to you. I am repeating her message. It is not ethical for a civilized man to enter the heart of an innocent girl by force and to run away from her. It is a wonder that still that big-eyed girl wants to give her body along with the heart to that thief. She is burning in the fire of physical passion. If you wish then I shall say something that will help both of you."

Kamlākar replied, "Your words do describe the pathetic condition of your friend in love, console me and simultaneously generate fear. You are the only option left for us. So, please do the needful."

Mālati said, "I'll secretly bring Anangmanjari to the garden of her house. You wait her outside. Then somehow I will clear the way and allow you to enter inside. Thus you two will meet." Mālati explained him the plan. She returned and narrated the incident to her friend. Night set in. Kamlākar thought, "Leaving the pond beauty has come to me." Kamlākar then got ready in best clothes and ornaments like a pond of lilies, slowly came to the gate of the garden very eager to meet his beloved. Anangmanajrai spent her day in expectation and doubt. In the evening, Mālati brought her to the garden by playing some tricks. She made her sit and wait under a mango tree. She went out and traced Kamlākar and secretly brought him inside the garden. As a traveller looks longingly at the shaded light that comes through the dense leaves of thickly standing trees, Kamlākar saw Anangmanjari through the boughs of a leafy tree. He was going towards her but she was so impassioned with the desire to make love that she ran shamelessly towards him and embraced him hard, "O that has stolen my heart! I have caught you now. You would not go anywhere else." The intensity of passion increased beyond her power of tolerance. She became breathless and stopped breathing. She died instantaneously; and fell on the ground as if she was a tender uprooted plant.

Kamlākar felt the loss and screamed, "Oh God! What has happened?" His ecstasy took off his energy. He too fainted. But regained senses in a few minutes. He took the body of that dead beloved in his lap, embraced it and kissed her again and again. He cried aloud. His agony grew. The pain was unbearable. The valves of his heart burst. He too died. The dead body of the lovers was lying there.

In the morning, the gardeners found the dead bodies and informed the master. The members of both the families felt ashamed at the incident. They were aggrieved for they had special fascination for their children. They sat there with the heads bowed low.

It so happened that Mani Vermā, Anangmanjari's husband, too came there from Tāmralipti to meet his wife. At his father-in-law's place he got the sad news. He wept and thinking deeply over the sudden demise of his beloved wife he came and saw her dead body. His pain grew and he too died there.

All the family members were crying bitterly. It was a strange sight and the story was interesting. The city dwellers also came there to get some firsthand information and to console the bereaved families.

The father of Anangmanjari was first to react. He went to the idol of Goddess Durgā. Many people stood behind him. With folded hands they prayed to the Goddess, "O Mother! This merchant Arthadatta, who established your idol here, has always been your devotee. So, please be kind to him."

The Goddess heard the request of her devotees. She is always ready to rescue her devotees. She blessed, "When passion subsides, these three should come alive."

With the blessing, the passions subsided and they awoke up as if from a sleep. All were happy. Kamlākar was ashamed of his deeds. With bowed head he returned to his house. Arthadatta also took his modest but dishonoured daughter and son-in-law and happily entered his house.

After finishing the story, Vetāla asked, "O Emperor! Who is the greatest fool among the three who died for love? If you would not answer despite knowing it then remember the previous curse, your head would be shattered into pieces."

Vikram answered, "O Yogeswar! Mani Vermā is the greatest fool among them. He knew that his wife was not sincere to him, that she had fallen in love with another person. He found her dead with another person. Yet in place of being angry with her he was so infatuated to her that he abandoned his life."

Vetāla heard it and vanished from his shoulder, and went to the tree where he resided. Without getting bewildered from the supernatural and magical show of Vetāla, the king moved forward to take him to the Monk, that very night.

and business system.

prepared and maintained about the products and the important

affected by changing seasons.

in order to maintain the smooth running of a business and in to cure it.

appear to be strength.

> '*To keep life at the top; planning must precede execution; below it is distribution; and at the root of everything is collection.*'

21

The executives at every stage must show healthy progress;
They must avoid abrupt changes causing downfall and disgrace;
Whether producing less or more than the capacity or demand:
They should not wait and ask for a favour or grant a grace.

The Story of Vishnuswāmi

King Vikram Sen reached that rosewood tree and picked up the human corpse with laughing Vetāla in it, put it up on his shoulder and walked silently towards the Buddha Monk.

The Vetāla in the dead body said, "O Emperor! You are gentle, humble and courageous. So, I'm telling you a unique story."

There was a city named Kusumpur ruled by King Dharaniwarāha. His kingdom had a number of Brahmins. There was a village called Brahmasthal in his kingdom. A Brahmin named Vishnuswāmi lived there. His wife was Swāhā and they had four sons.

Time passed. The parents died and the relatives usurped the properties of the four brothers. The brothers discussed their predicament internally and came to the conclusion, "We have no future in this place. We should go to some other place." Having discussed the matter they came to Yagyasthal, the place of their maternal uncle. Their grandfather had died but the maternal uncles helped them. They lived there and started their studies.

As time passed their expenses too grew. It became difficult for the maternal uncles to support them. They started insulting them every now and then.

Vishnuswāmi's sons were agitated at the regular insults being hurled by their relatives. They again discussed the matter and as expected escapism was their choice. The elder brother called them at a lonely place and said,

"Brothers! What should we do? You can take it as the deeds of destiny. A man cannot do anything anywhere in this world. Today, I was very restless and moved aimlessly and reached a forest. There I saw an old man lying dead and unattended. I thought that he was lucky to have died. He has now no burden to bear. Out of despair, I made a knot in a tree and tried to kill myself. But I fainted and the old rope ruptured. I fell down. When I regained my senses I saw a kind man trying to give me breath. He told me, 'Friend! Although you are learned yet why are you so worried. Men of good deeds live happily while the men of bad deeds fall in pain. If you are suffering from some pain then be good and perform good deeds. Why are you throwing yourself to hell by committing suicide.' He said so and consoled me; went away. I threw the idea of suicide from my mind and came here. If destiny does not cooperate then one can't even die. I am thinking of going on a penance so that I may not be poor again."

The other brothers replied, "Arya! Why do the learned are sad even in poverty. They should not be. Don't they know that wealth is always active? It's never static. Accumulated wealth becomes meaningless at the end. Like friendship of wicked persons or prostitutes wealth never stay with anyone. So, an active learned man should learn to do something rare so that the wealth can come as and when needed."

When the brothers suggested like that, the elder brother queried, "What quality can we develop?" Then they decided to wander and learn some science. They designated a place to meet again and dispersed in different directions to learn some rare science.

Years passed. The four brothers met at the designated place. They started asking each other, "What have you learnt?"

One said, "I have learnt the science of creating flesh on the bones of a dead being."

The second said, "I have learnt the science of creating skin and hair according to the bone of a living being if it has flesh on it."

The third said, "I have learnt the science of creating eyes, nose and other organs if a living being has flesh and skin, etc."

The fourth said, "I have learnt the science of giving life to a living being if it has a body and his organs."

Now they were ready to test the science of one another. They went to a forest to search for bones. As destiny sought, they found the bones of a lion. Without thinking about the living being whose bones they were taking they brought the bones of the dead lion.

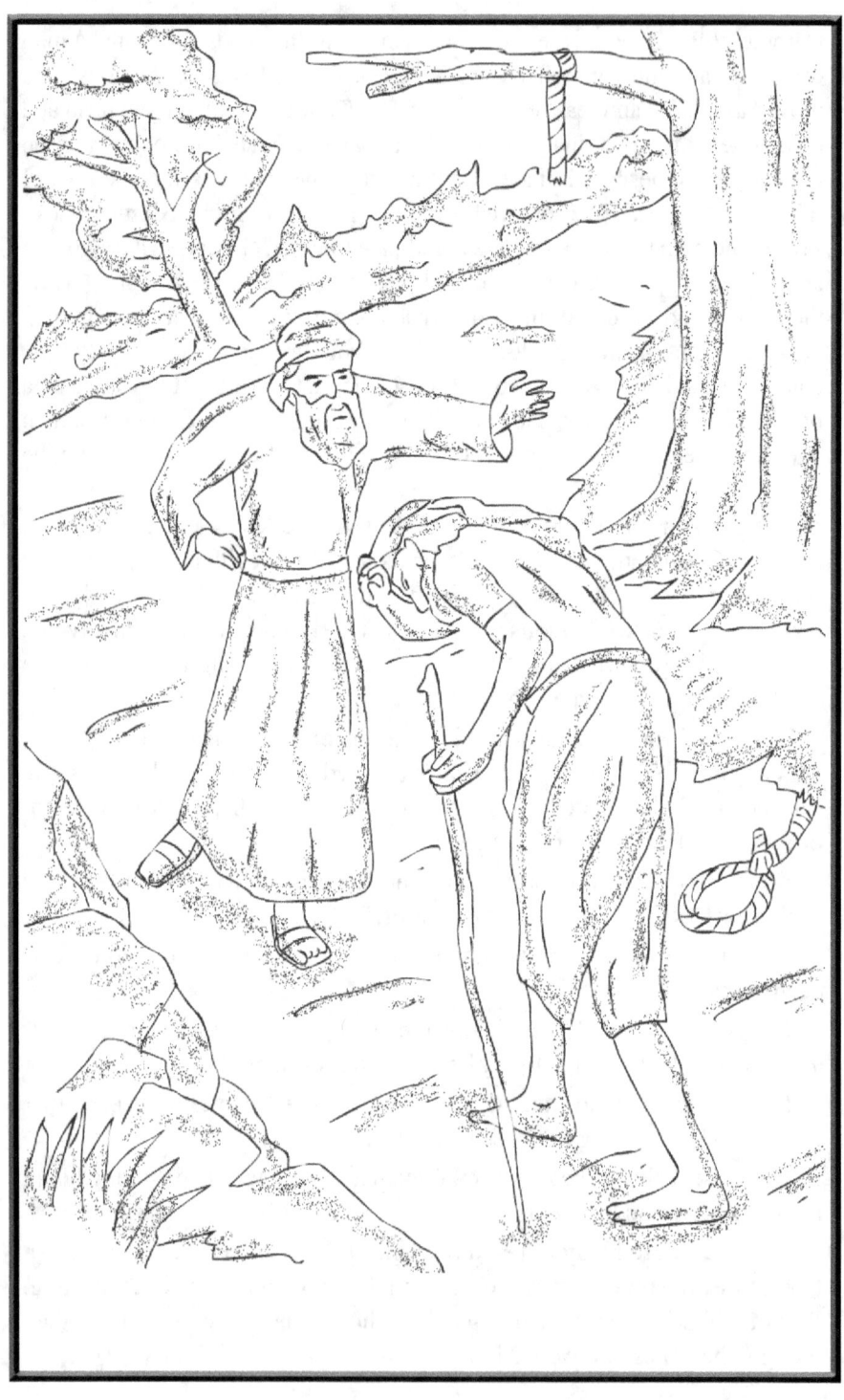

One of them covered and united the bones with flesh. The second one created skin and hair on it. The third one gave him all the organs. Now the lion was ready. The fourth one gave life to it.

The lion came alive. It had mane around its neck. It had sharp teeth and large dreadful mouth. It had sharp nails. The dreadful creature rose and killed all the four brothers that had given life to it. After killing them it went inside the dense forest.

In this way, the sons of the Brahmin were killed because they had committed the crime of giving life to a lion. No one can be happy after giving life to wicked. If the destiny goes wrong then the hard earned knowledge also fails to give wealth. It turns deadly. After finishing the story, Vetāla asked the king, "O Emperor! Who is the greatest criminal among the four brothers who created the lion? Remember the already given curse."

Vikram answered, "He is the sinner who gave life to the lion. The other three who created flesh, skin, hair and organs are not culprits, as they did not know about the animal. But the fourth one saw the dead lion and gave it life just to show the power of his knowledge that too without taking any precaution. He is responsible for Brahma-hatyā (the killing of Brahmins)."

Vetāla heard it and vanished from his shoulder, and went to the tree where he resided. The king again moved forward to take him to the Monk, that very night.

the top secrets of the company.

fe.

dge.

In

'Wise counseling helps one to come out of dense dark woods; and foolish advices annihilate in no time.'

22

The goal before them is incessant growth, they apprehend,
Achievement is the result of work and spirit they blend,
Many mysterious gains easily come an executive's way
For evolution and improvement till the end is their end.

The Story of Devasoma

King Vikram Sen again reached that rosewood tree and picked up the human corpse with laughing Vetāla in it. He put it up on his shoulder and walked faster but silently towards the Buddha Monk. The Vetāla in the dead body said, "O Rajendra! King of Kings! Indra among the Kings! There is obduracy in your act of carrying me again and again. Anyway, I'm telling you a new story to keep you fresh." Saying so, Vetāla started the following story.

In the kingdom of Kalinga, there was a city named Shobhāwati. In that heaven like city only virtuous people resided. King Pradyumna, who was famous for extraordinary valour, ruled there. In the kingdom there was a village called Yagyasthal inhabited by the Brahmins. In the village there was an Agnihotri Brahmin named Yagyasoma who was well versed in the Vedas and worshipped the guests and gods. His wife was worthy to him. In old age she gave birth to a son. The father fostered him with great care and perfection. As a result he grew wise and imbibed all virtuous qualities. He was very loving to his parents. He was given a name Devasoma.

At the age of sixteen he was well versed and very humble. He attracted all. All loved him. But unfortunately, he died out of high fever. The parents cried out in agony. They embraced the dead body and did not give it for cremation. The body was not put into pyre and fire. The people of the place explained to him, advised him and persuaded him by saying, "O Brahmin! You know the good and the bad, and yet do you not know the forms created by clouds in the sky that last only for a few minutes? Don't you know the celestial system of the world? The kings who led a luxurious life thinking themselves to be immortal, they all were put on the pyre and burnt in fire or they were eaten away by Time or jackals? No one could stop them. Then, what can be said about others? O Learned man! What will you do by embracing this dead body?"

He heard the old men and the relatives and realized the futility of trying to save the dead body. He agreed for cremation. A pyre was prepared. All the men of the village participated in this journey to the burning *ghāta*. In that burning *ghāta* a Shiva-like Mendicant was living and did great penance. He had a hut as hermitage. He was in old age; very lean and thin. The nerves were out as if they had tied the skin and flesh and stopping them from falling off. He had yellow matted hair. That Mendicant heard the clamour and uproar outside. He asked one of his disciples who was expert in using abusive language, and used to carry *tumri* (wooden or gourd vessel used by seers), "Child! Why are the people creating uproar? Go out and return fast after knowing the cause. I have never heard such an uproar before."

The preceptor said so but the disciple denied, "I won't go. You may go yourself. It's my lunchtime. I'm already late."

The guru chided him, "O Fool! O gluttonous! Contempt to your life! Fie! Fie! Half of the day has hardly gone past, how is that it is your lunchtime?" Hearing the chiding, the wicked disciple bluntly replied to his guru, "O old, decayed and sunken man! Contempt to you! Neither I'm your disciple nor you my preceptor. I'll go to some other place. Carry your own *tumri*." He showed anger and left the stick and the vessel behind and went out.

Smiling on his fate the Mendicant came out of the hut and went there where the body of the young boy was kept for cremation. The crowd was mourning the death of the child. The old *yogi* decided to enter the dead body of the young boy. He returned to the loneliness of his hut. He wept very loudly and then he started dancing with the correct movement of hands and legs. After a few moments the *Yogi* in order to experience the youthful days again with his acquired mystic power left the old and weathered out body and entered that body of the son of the Brahmin. Suddenly, the young boy rose up and sat down on the pyre. They all cried, "He is alive, he is alive. By good fortune he is alive."

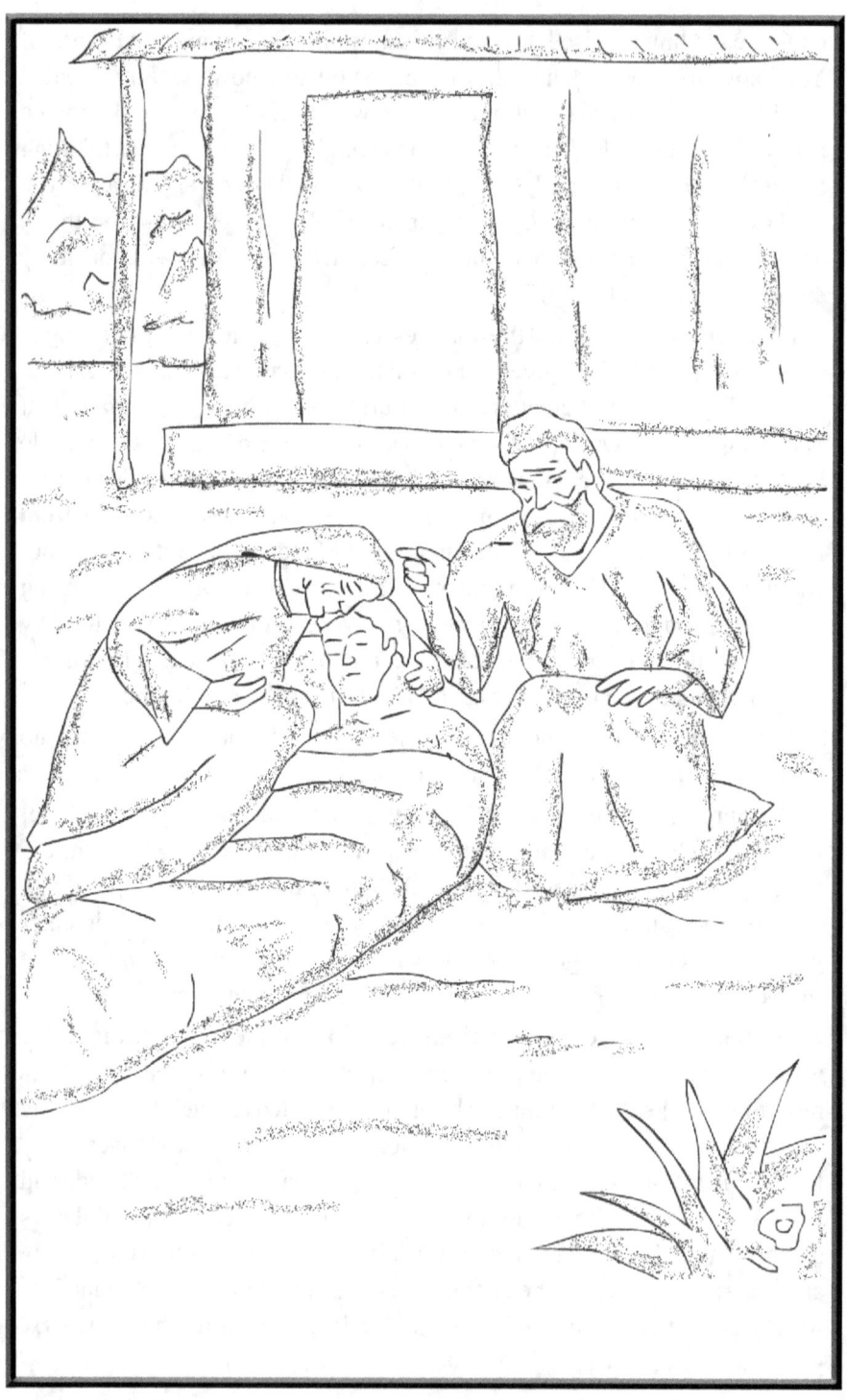

The Mendicant in the body of that Brahmin youth said to his relatives, "I went to heaven. Lord Shankar gave me life on a condition that I will go for penance to perfect *'Mahāpāshupata Vrata'*. I have to obey his order. I have to go immediately to a lonely place and start the penance otherwise I won't be alive. So, people should return. I am also departing."

He made the relatives understand the urgency of the Mahāvrata and sent them back. He returned to throw his own dead body in a ditch and proceeded as a young man to some unknown place to start the penance afresh.

After finishing the story, Vetāla asked the king, "O Emperor! Tell me why did the Mendicant first wept loudly and then danced. I'm very curious to know it."

Vikram answered, "Listen to me, O Vetāla! The Mendicant thought that his parents loved his body during his childhood and it was that body which gave him perfection in mysterious sciences. He was leaving that useful body. It should not have been abandoned. But he was leaving that. That is why he first wept loudly. Then he thought that in a new and young body he would be able to go for greater penance and master up many more things. So, out of ecstatic joy he danced."

Vetāla heard it and vanished from his shoulder, and went to the tree where he resided. King Vikram also moved forward to take him to the Monk, that very night.

characteristic of director independence.

gains.

Most of the businessmen and the men in management are

kept intact.

and from human resources to other resources.

better than repetition.

'Management is an art and never a science. Scientific management does not mean management of science or management by science. It means keeping an eye on everything; and growing well and with all; and getting refreshed when tired.'

23

An executive thinks faster when he sits idle,
Solves economic tangles and financial riddle,
Makes everyone move as he wishes to, for
He is never at an end but always in the saddle.

A Mother and Her Daughter

King Vikram in the dead darkness of the moonless night came to the burning *ghāta* and reached that rosewood tree to pick up the human corpse with laughing Vetāla in it. He lifted the dead body to his shoulder; walked faster yet silently towards the Buddha Monk. Then the Vetāla said, "O Emperor! I'm tired of this coming and going. Yet you are not agitated. I have been telling you different stories. Now, I'm asking you a difficult question."

In the ancient time, among the Southern Countries, there was a prominent king who ruled twelve states. He was called Manaleswar (the king of a Region). His name was Dharma and wife was Chandrāwati. She gave birth to a daughter Lāwanyawati. When the girl crossed the age of puberty, the king started thinking about her marriage. Unfortuntaely, that time his relatives conspired against him; dethroned him and broke the kingdom into many parts.

The deposed king Dharma was facing threat to his life too. So, he decided to escape. One night he collected all precious jewels and left the kingdom in the company of his wife and daughter. They moved towards Mālava, the country of his father-in-law and expected security there. Along with his wife and daughter he reached the Mountain Range of Vindhyāchala. In hear and pain somehow he spent the night in the forest.

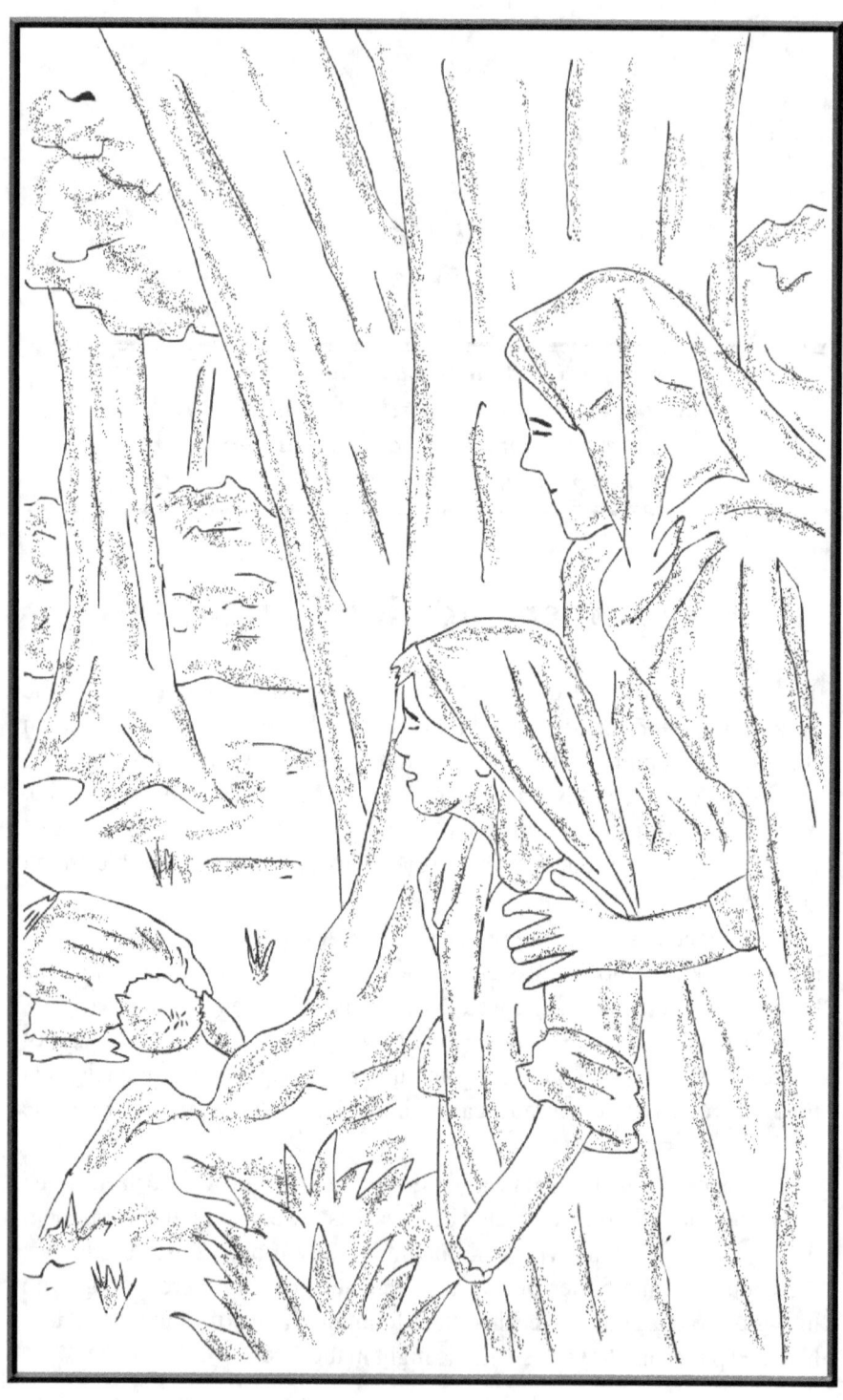

In the morning, the sun rose up in the eastern sky. It was real danger to proceed ahead as the region is infested with thieves and robbers. But the king had no other option. He moved on foot with fear-stricken wife and daughter in that region of Bheels (rough tribal people) and other wild men who robbed and killed travellers. The area had few gentlemen. The king entered a village. The robbers saw a rich king coming towards them. They took up arms and ran towards him. The king told his wife and daughter, "They are inhuman. They should not touch you. For safety please enter the dense forest."

Out of fear the queen entered the forest with her daughter Lāwanyawati. The king was left alone to fight the tribal robbers. The king carried his sword and shield but chose to attack the robbers with bow and arrow. He released the arrows so fast that it seemed to be the rain of arrows. He killed many robbers. But their master directed them to intensify the attack in unison. They were many. The king was fatally injured and killed in the fight. The robbers took away his wealth and fled.

The queen Chandāwati, with her daughter Lāwanywati, saw the attack from behind the bushes and the King getting killed. They kept moving slowly in the dark and dense forest. She wept and entered another forest. Soon it was noon. The sun grew hot. It was time for the mother and daughter to take shelter under the shade of a tree. They saw a pond. They sat down under a shade to take rest.

It so happened that a king named Chandsigh, very rich and living in near vicinity came with his son to the forest for hunting. He noticed the track made by the feet of the queen Chandāwati and daughter Lāwanywati. Chandsingh said to his son Singhaparākrama, "O son! If we follow the tracks of these beautiful feet having the signs of royalty, we can get the women; then accept one that you like as your wife."

His son, Singhaparākrama replied, "There are the tracks of smaller feet. She is fit for becoming my wife but the other tracks are that of larger feet, she must be elder. She will be suitable for you. You should marry her."

Chandsingh heard his son and said, "O son! What are you talking about? Your mother died before my eyes. I have no desire for another woman when I have lost such a good wife."

The son had his own logic and said, "O father! Don't say like that. The house of a master is empty when there is no wife. You must have heard the statement of Mooladeva that where there is no woman with bulging breasts and smooth round thighs to wait for a man, that house is like a jail. Who would be foolish enough to enter such a jail? So, O father! I give you the oath of my life that if you won't accept what I have selected just now as your wife then I'll kill myself."

The father had no option but to agree to his son. He did not wish to lose his son. They agreed to marry the two women if they get them: the woman of smaller feet with the son and of larger feet with the father.

The two followed the track and came to the pond. There they saw Chandrāwati glowing with beauty and attraction. Out of sheer curiosity they came to her. She thought him to be a thief. She hurriedly got up. But her wise daughter said, "It is meaningless to be afraid of them. They are not thieves. They are well built and have pleasing personality. They are definitely amateur hunters who have come for hunting in the forest."

In the meantime, Chandsingh had reached there. He came down of the horse and said, "O Beauty! Don't get worried. We have come for hunting here. Have faith on us and without any fear and doubt tell us who are you? It seems that you have come to the forest as Rati and Preeti in desolation and in pain of separation after Kāmdev was burnt by the third eye of Lord Shiva. Why have you entered this uninhabited forest? Your body is adapted to live in the houses of jewels. Why have you brought down your beautiful feet in this thorny place? They should move in wide and smooth courtyard. We are deeply aggrieved to see you in such pathetic condition. We cannot tolerate your presence in this forest inhabited by wild beasts."

The queen took a long breath to hear the consoling words of Chandsingh. Perplexed at the agonizing situation, slowly she narrated everything that happened to her in short leaving out all the details. When she finished her tale Chandsingh encouraged her with sweet words. He knew her to be without a husband. He accepted her along with her daughter. On the horse back they brought them to their city that was rich like the city of Kuber, the god of wealth. They had got a new lease of life after desperately moving in the forest. The queen too accepted them, as she had no choice left.

The queen Chandrāwati had smaller feet so she was married to the son, Singhparākrama, and the daughter who had larger feet was married to Chandsingh. True men never break the promise made earlier.

This way because of the opposite size of their feet the mother and daughter became the wife of the son and father. The daughter became the mother-in-law and the mother became the daughter-in-law. In due course of time both the mother and daughter gave birth to many sons and daughters.

After finishing the story, Vetāla asked the king, who was moving fearlessly in the night, "O Emperor! What will be the relation between the sons and daughter of the daughter with the sons and daughters of the mother who were so married to the son and the father?"

Vikram was silent. He heard every bit of it, with intent concentration. But the King thought he could not explain the relation among the children. The change in status had changed everything. The king kept mum. He did not say anything. He kept on moving silently

Vetāla laughed silently and thought that it is the most difficult question. The king can't answer it. No one can answer it. This type of peculiar situation arises once in million years. That is why he is moving silently. He cannot deceive me because of the effect of the curse. I am pleased with the tremendous courage of this valiant man. So, today, I will deceive that wicked Buddha Monk and give his desired divine power to this great king."

Having thought like that and after coming to a final decision the Vetāla said to the king, "O Emperor! You seem to be pleased despite moving to and fro in the dead darkness of night and in a burning *ghāta*. You have no hesitation. I am satisfied with your patience and am in wonder. Now, you can take this dead body. I shall go out of it. And, now I'm telling you what is beneficial to you. That wicked person for whom you are carrying this dead body will call me into this body and worship me. With an intention to sacrifice you, he will ask you to prostrate on the ground. O Emperor! Say to that wicked person like this, 'I don't know how to prostrate. First do and show it to me, then I will repeat it.' Then he will show you how to prostrate by falling on the ground. The moment he drops to the ground chop his head off. Then all the *siddhi* (perfection) and *aiswarya* (wealth) of the Vidyādhars (Genie) will be yours. If you will fail to do so, the Monk will sacrifice you and will get everything that he wishes to get. That is the reason that I have delayed you so much. I had to be sure. May you get perfection! Now, go." Saying so, Vetāla came out of the dead body and went somewhere.

The king thought over the matter: what Vetāla had said and what the Monk was doing or was to do that very night. He too planned his course of action and carried the dead body on his shoulder and happily moved towards the big banyan tree.

Note:

The question posed by Vetāla has not been answered. Although, it is a peculiar and rare situation, it needs to be clarified.

The name of the family-tradition is obviously male dominated. So, the writer says that the mother became a daughter-in-law and the daughter became mother-in-law. If and once, this relationship is established then there is no problem in deciding the relation among their children. They should not be treated as the children of the mother or the daughter. They should be treated as the children of the father and the son; and hence, their relation will be decided accordingly.

Of course, in our society relations are established both ways; from the side of the wife as well as the side of the husband. So, it is complicated but in one house one type of relationship exists and continues and since, both the mother and the daughter are living under the same roof so the relation will be maintained according to the relation of the father and the son. Therefore, the children of the father would be elders to the children of the son. And, since there is no chance of the children returning to their maternal house, so there will not be complication. They won't be asked or forced to declare their internal relationship. Moreover, what is once established is established forever. It's a simple matter of the way we think and at the place we live.

cases.

of management to pass a message so that the message reaches more

their commitments to others: kings, businessmen or mass. There

obeyed.

being crushed.

different groups of products because one company is producing

Both the things are important: to take a decision and to stick to that decision. The fact is that once a decision is taken a person bankruptcy. It is true both for the entrepreneurs and the Directors

'Be it management, life, the earth or the universe, there is a way to every place from everywhere. One starts moving and gets his way; one keeps moving and fi nally reaches the destination.'

Epilogue

Victorious Vikram

With the weighty dead body on his shoulder Vikram reached the Buddha Monk Shāntisheela, who was waiting for him in that dark moonless night, sitting amidst the trees. The King came near the Monk. Near the fierce-looking monk was a ritualistic pitcher full of blood; the lamps were burning with human intestines; the fire burning with offerings; the essential materials for worship and sacrifice were ready and the Monk was sitting at the centre of a circle drawn with the white powder of human bones.

The Monk got up and said to the king, "O Emperor! You have obliged me by doing a great but difficult job. There is no one like you. Who can accomplish such a difficult task? What a deadly time and dangerous place! The people truly say that you are great among the kings and of high family order. You have not cared for your life but finished the work for another person. Those do that are really great. This is the greatness in great men that they will not deviate from the accepted task."

The Monk said so and took off the dead body from his shoulder. He bathed the dead body, put a garland around his neck and placed at the centre of the circle. Then he smeared sacred ash all over his body and wore the sacred thread made up of hair and sat motionless for sometime in meditation. During that period he called Vetāla and made him enter the dead body with the power of his mediation and the force of his penance.

The Monk then started the worship of Vetāla. First he sprinkled holy water taken from the human skull; then offered new and bright white teeth as flowers; fragrant sandal like red blood; he placed human eye as incense stick; and the human flesh as *naivedya* (food) and completed the worship in the ritualistic way practised by such wicked and demonic *tāntrics* who use special *mantras* for devious ends.

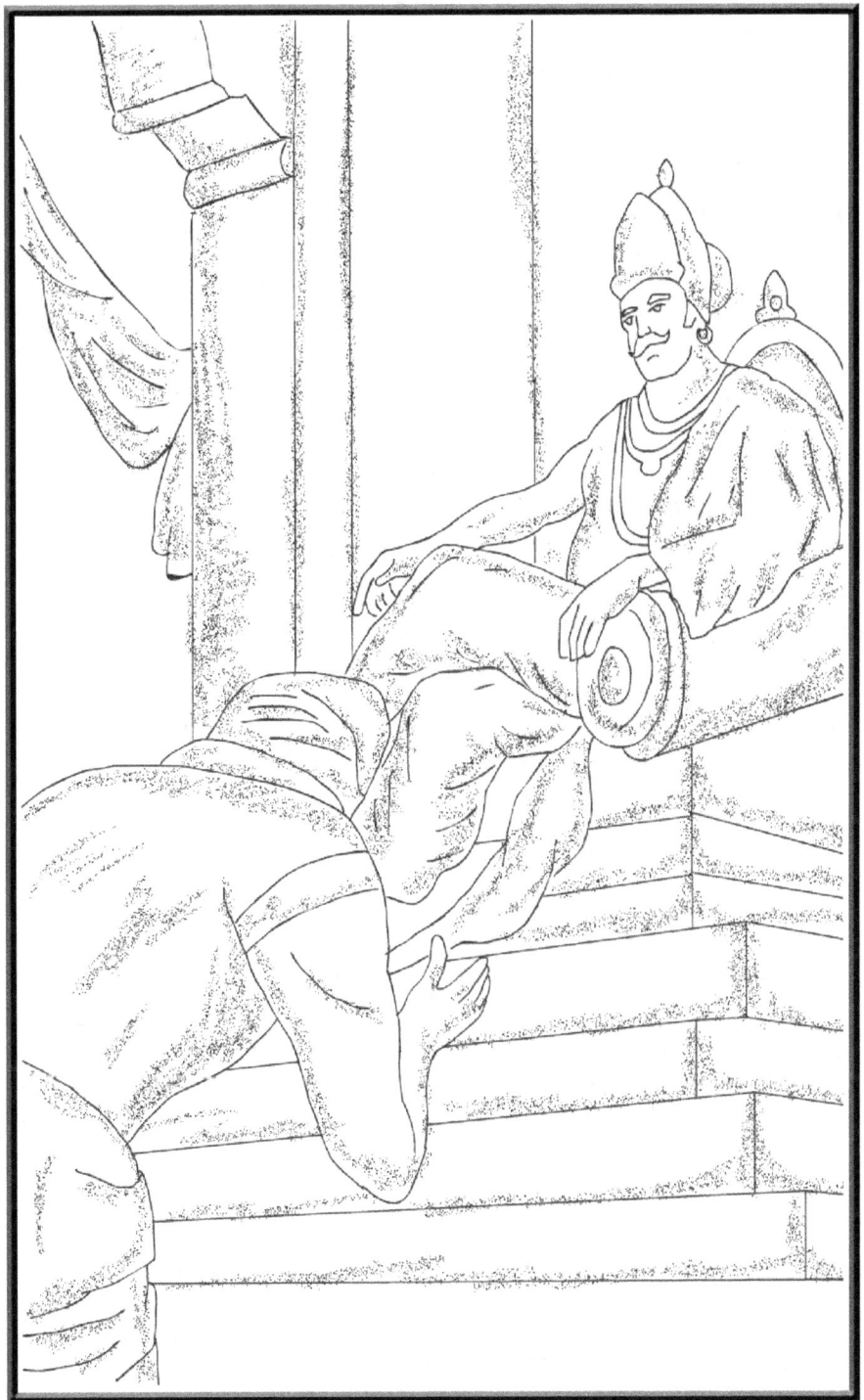

When the worship was complete, the Monk told the king, "O Emperor! The master of all Mantras has appeared here. Prostrate before him to salute him with all your eight parts. In that way, he will fulfill your desires."

The King remembered the words of Vetāla and said to the Monk, "Gentleman! I don't know such a kind of salutation. First do it and show me, then I will repeat and do the same."

The Monk prostrated before the Vetāla in the dead body to show how such salutations are performed. As soon as he bent before Vetāla, the king took out his sword and chopped off his head. He tore open his chest and took out the lotus like heart. Then he offered that head and that lotus heart to Vetāla.

Happy ghosts appeared from all sides. Vetāla was completely satisfied with the performance of the king. He told the King from the dead body, "O Emperor! This Monk had the desire to be the king of Vidyādhars (Genie). Now you will get that after you have enjoyed the kingship on the earth."

The king said, "O Yogindra! If you are pleased then every desire will be fulfilled. I don't speak without purpose. I'm asking you to bless these stories, which conclude with the 25th episode and become famous all over the earth and get respect."

Vetāla heard the request from the king and said, "O Emperor! As you wish! It will be popular and earn respect. And, I am adding something special. Listen! The person who will read these or tell these 24 stories will fulfill the desire along with this 25th will be purged from all sins. The place where these stories will be told and the person or persons who will listen to these stories will not be infested with Yakshas, Rakshasas, Dākinies, Vetālas, Kushumānds, and Brahmarākshasas. They will not be able to create their effect there." Vetāla said so and with his magical power came out of that dead body and returned to his abode.

Soon Lord Shankar appeared there with his aides called *Ganas*. The king bowed to him and saluted him. The Lord ordered the king, "Child! You have done a great thing by killing this wicked recluse who wished to be the undisputed king of Vidyādhars. With my power and order you will destroy the demons who have taken birth with wicked intentions. I now christen you as **Vikramāditya** to demolish the wicked, oppressive, mischievous, vicious and licentious beings. So, you will control the whole earth including islands and *pātāla* and be the king of Vidyādhars. There you will enjoy everything. Now take this Sword from me, known as *Aparājita* meaning invincible, indomitable or formidable. You can conquer whatever you wish with the power of this Sword."

For the blessings bestowed, Vikram sang in praise of the Lord and pleased him; the Lord then returned to his abode.

Conclusion

Now, everything was over. There was no work left for Vikram who was renamed as Vikramāditya by Lord Shankar. The night changed into morning. The king returned to his city and entered the palace. The people burst into festivities and felicitated their King Vikramāditya. He regaled in their joy but spent the day in worshipping Lord Shankar, in charity; in music and dance.

Within a short period, King Vikramāditya conquered all the islands and *pātāla* too with the grace of Lord Shankar. He ruled for a very long period on the earth and enjoyed every possible pleasure.

After that he got the great prosperity of the Vidyādhars and ruled and enjoyed that life also for a very long period. At last, the King on his own returned to Lord Shankar and was granted Salvation.

countries.

and respected product.

Management.

'Growth, Procreation and Continuity are three distinguishing features of living beings. Lively management grows, shows branching and continues to enjoy greater prosperity.'

Conclusion

Vikram Favours Quality to Quantity

The title of this conclusion of the book may mislead the readers. So it must be clarified. There is no doubt that Vikram favours or favoured 'Quality to Quantity' but it is not only Vikram who favours 'Quality'; all people do, especially those who have a bit of wisdom and refinement.

It is the 'Quality' of life, of management, health and also of happiness that all the people are fighting for. Research is being conducted to improve the quality and utility of products. Books are being written, produced, sold, bought, read and followed to improve the quality. In fact, this book is also written with the sole aim of improving the quality of Management and Life: life of management, life in management or to be very accurate, of life through management. So, the readers should never feel that only Vikram favours or favoured quality.

It is said that originally Lord Shiva told these stories to Goddess Pārvati in a temple. Vetāla secretly overheard it. For this offence he was punished by the Lord to be a Vetāla. So, these stories are didactic in substance.

Exaggerations

In these stories there are exaggerations. It seems that exaggerations must have been added by different narrators during the Middle Ages either to enhance its effect or to diminish its value. One obvious exaggeration is about rumours that the Buddha Monk Shāntisheel needed to offer one thousand heads of kings. He had already sacrificed 999 and King Vikram was the 1000th and the last.

But it may not be true and is unbelievable. It cannot be the statement of such a writer who had reasoned out so many exquisite things and complicated situations. The number of 1000 kingdoms and kings are always doubtful. Moreover, it is not possible to kill 999 kings without being detected.

No sane person can believe the killing of so many kings for sacrifice. So, the stories have depicted only successful merchants who have accumulated wealth, are religious and charitable in spirit, show kindness and hospitality. Along with them there are the kings, princes and princesses, ministers, employees, sons, daughters and other men and woman. But everywhere, Vikram prefers and favours quality over quantity; the strong inner and moral character to accumulation of wealth.

Stories from the Golden Period

The stories belong to the golden period of Indian history when there was all round prosperity, diligence, intelligence and hence riches. There was no poverty. The so-called poor worked so hard and sincerely that they earned enough to fulfill their physical needs. There was no craving for more and more. Hence, the people were happy. Their unhappiness was their own creation or the working of fate or natural calamity.

The family of the washer man too is rich in inner wealth and moral character. They too had the guts to sacrifice their life. The killings and terror of criminals were never there. If present, they would be crushed brutally.

Untimely death happened mostly on the battlefield. Now, that battlefield has changed into conspiracies. Valour is gone and replaced by cunningness that is a major cause of pain and restless in modern society. A very common dialogue comes, "Everyone is corrupt." It is not true but so many persons are corrupt hence, it is difficult to refute the charge and prove that most of us are still honest and sincere. If not then how the society is surviving. Society survives only on intelligence, diligence and sincerity of greater percentage of people; and not on the selected conspirators and criminals or their godfathers. They have a very short lifespan of only 6 to 8 years. No criminal has survived for more than that period.

One thing is very common among them. They are all very watchful. They assess the person before communicating with them or before offering hospitality or calling them to their residence. Precautions are assets in the sense that the alert person will never face grief.

Root and Rootlessness

Earning of money is good but it will not show prosperity if the accumulated wealth is being lost. Prosperity is delicate. It comes only when the contact with the root is unbroken; if the boughs are not broken and if there are no loopholes. That person can never prosper if he loses what his ancestors have collected and saved. The sap from the root will keep the leaves at the top green, full of green pigments and chlorophyll. It will keep the plant green and blooming: flowering and bearing fruit. In this way traditions must be maintained for modernity. Modernity cannot grow in air and remain intact in air.

The persons who have strong desire to fly with an airplane wish to come down to earth from the moment they are high up in the air. Ground is solid and roots are full of sap. These two things are the beginning of the green and healthy way to prosperity.

The greatest problem about human beings is that their thinking is getting narrowed down. They are not considering other aspects of life, other living beings and non-living things, the ecology and Nature, natural resources and natural phenomon. They are reading the so-called books, which are on only one thing; and they are being taught by the so-called experts who are masters of only one subject and ciphers in others. Even when they know about other things, they lack confidence and are afraid of giving vent to known facts, own ideas or to a certain extent, established truth. In modern world, there is hardly any capital punishment.

On the other hand, on many occasions criminals are rewarded. This sends a wrong message to the society. As a result *the best lack all conviction/ While the worst are full of passionate intensity.* For better society, greater gain, happier life and all round development, healthy management is needed: both of natural resources and human resources.

It is very unfortunate that both are being wasted: man has no work; and all the hidden strength and vitality of the earth is being mined out. **Modern management must look at all and take everything into consideration. Only looking after the self is not enough.**

Human Resource Development or Utilisation

The word Human Resource Development is misleading. Of course, an organization must arrange training courses and impart adequate training to its employees but the prime concern of modern management is the Utilization of Human Resource, and not its development. An organization must appoint able and experienced staff for better and efficient work and healthier growth. The main aim is to utilize the knowledge and skill and dexterity (both the apparent and latent abilities) that an aspirant or an employee possesses so that the works can be smoothly completed and the targets achieved. The difference between development and utilization must be kept in mind. If the employees lack a bit of this or that then it should be given through periodical training; and it is always a pleasure if the employees are gaining in experience and growing well. It is always advantageous and beneficial to an organization. Educational Institutions, Training Centres and other such organization are different. The management is also a part of general management but through the ages they have never been treated as business organization while many business houses have invested in the field of education and training. Yet the difference remains between an educational institution and a commercial institution.

Investment and Fruits

At a first glance one cannot realise what is paying and what is not. Jewels may appear like simple fruits and a fruit may have been stuffed with jewels. While choosing and deciding a trade or selecting a field for investment or reinvestment, care has to be taken to assess the fruit; the return from the investment; the paying capacity in the field or concerned trade.

It is not a big problem if it has been a family business because a lot is already known, particularly problems, nuisances and returns. But if it is a new field then the men, merchants and organizations of that field must be studied carefully before opting for or against it.

Take the example of Vikram and the Buddha Monk Shāntisheel. Vikram would not have been attracted towards the Monk and his penance or desire or work, had there been no jewels in the fruits. He knew how many jewels the Monk had already invested. The work must be important and fruitful. The overall returns from the work must be more than hundred times. Otherwise, there is no meaning in such a huge investment.

Parts and the Whole

That knowledge will be imperfect if one knows only the pupils of the eyes or the secretion from the eyes or the ailments and cure of eyes. Actually, the valid knowledge must be the knowledge of complete human physiology; its working; its different organs and systems and the knowledge why all the different systems become one system; and body's relation with others: the living and non-living as life depends on all.

In management, neither management nor the knowledge of management is limited to financial management or to sales management. Management is that complete whole; and one must be sure, *the whole contains a lot and numerous things*. Yet, the whole is related to and depends on many other and non-aligned things and phenomenon that may not have anything to do directly with management.

Because of this single track thinking and racing in a one way channel, we are getting something and missing a lot; we are moving with some but a lot more are left (ahead, behind and by the side). So, no one is satisfied with what he has got. When at the end one weighs the accumulated wealth he finds that it is insignificant and weightless. He feels that the whole life has been wasted.

So live in a wider perspective, look in close vicinity and very far and wide, think in terms of all to know more, to think more, to get more, to possess more, to enjoy more and to live more. Just introspect, if a child is weeping in your close vicinity, can you eat your food? Can you enjoy the food? Will that food be rightly digested? Will that food give ample energy? Whosoever the child may be, it cannot be normal eating, digesting and converting into energy. Man has lost that energy; hence, there is no pleasure or peace in life and the whole exercise seems to be wasteful.

One should feel one's own organization is not everything; that the department he belongs to is not all; that whatever he does is not all; and whatever he produces is not enough. Life is infinite; ways are infinite; means are infinite; needs are infinite; everything is infinite; but the individual is mortal and perishable.

Only the individual will perish. He will live after death only because of others. So, others are more important than 'he'; his branch; his product; his strength; his wishes; his desires and his achievements.

One should not think that other things are different hence are unrelated and do not come under our purview. Such petty divisions are created for selfish gain. All are related and all are important: from an earthworm to an elephant; from a tiny mustard seed to a big jackfruit; from a pin to a bulldozer; from precious gems to simple packing. They can be ignored only at the cost of our own life, sustenance, growth and existence.

We do not know it and do not visualize it. All are integral part of everyone else. They affect our life, our organization and our management in many ways, mostly positive. We also affect them. *So, don't live in parts, live a full life; don't see the management divided, see it as a unified whole: very large, very big, very great and very essential.*

Man must co-mingle and co-exist. He cannot treat himself different from others. A person cannot survive merely on the basis of the products of his own organization or his own field. He needs many other things that will be given by others. That is how other organizations and other products become important. Family and social life is also a part of management. Manage it well for good living, happiness, growth, prosperity and for life to **continue.**

Temporary Arrangement and Permanent Management

Managing for a day or a year is different. In the former responsibilities are not very tough and the risk is not high.

All the stories of Vetāla are related to kings, queens, ministers, merchants, wise men and people of high ambitions. When the kings go out on definite purpose or on some errand, they hand over the kingdom to the minister or ministers. It is a temporary arrangement. But because they are permanent ministers and executive heads it is a sort of permanent arrangement too. They go out with complete assurance. It is not possible in modern day management when there are different departmental heads and managers. The absence of the chief will mean that the organization is lacking in focus and a central command.

Different divisions have made it difficult to make temporary arrangement and run the organization well. There are different aspects; even different divisions. In one set there are the chief, executives, controllers/ managers and workers; in another set comes: infrastructure, resources, administration and product.

In modern organization, there are numerous investors and they rightly expect good results and high returns. The crux of the situation is that the director/ the board of directors want more production; the subordinates want greater payment and more considerations; customers need better products and want faster delivery; competing organizations conspire for delay at every level; the board of advisers suggests change; employees resist change as they have adapted the way. Among all these conflicting vibes an organization feels suffocated.

There are three separate and sharp divisions in marketing: Distribution, Wholesale, and Retail. These three combined together are called 'distribution network'. Distribution has one or a few centres; wholesale is done mostly on regional basis but there are numerous retail outlets: from Malls and specialized shops to vendors and hawkers. The very width and length, the height and depth of business and business organizations suggest that it is not easy to manage an organization. The temporary success is shown only because of decentralization and division of responsibility is quite different from division of labour.

Consistent work for many busy, long and tiring years will give lasting name and fame, and thus durability to an organization. One will have to work diligently, intelligently and consistently for many years for reaching at the top and to remain there. Once at the top and then coming to middle, lower middle or at the bottom is neither success nor growth. It is general and common existence like birth-growth-death. There should be birth, growth and immortality or salvation. Only a long healthy and happy life can justify the hard work and just deeds: Endure hundred winters: *jiweda sharadah shatam.*

CAREER & BUSINESS MANAGEMENT
(कैरियर एण्ड बिजनेस मैनेजमेंट)

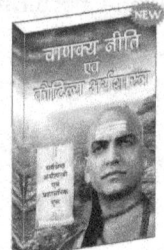

10222 P • ₹ 135 • 264 pp

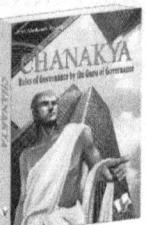

00701 P • ₹ 175 • 256 pp

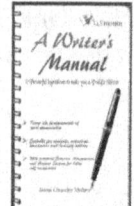

00201 P • ₹ 195 • 168 pp

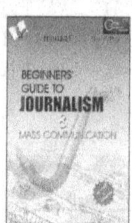

5621 D • ₹ 150 • 124 pp

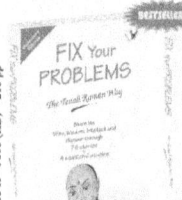

00203 H • ₹ 395 (EB) • 216 pp

00203 P • ₹ 150 • 228 pp

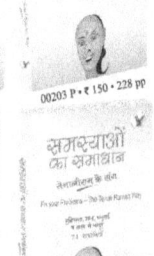
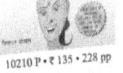

00211 P • ₹ 195 • 264 pp

10210 P • ₹ 135 • 228 pp

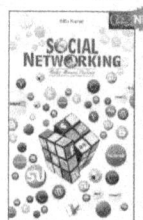

00703 P • ₹ 120 • 136 pp

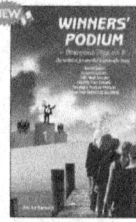

00604 P • ₹ 200 • 168 pp

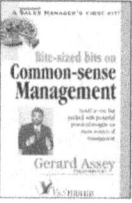

5636A • ₹ 150 • 256 pp

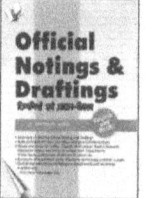

90702 P • ₹ 175 • 132 pp

STRESS MANAGEMENT (तनाव मुक्ति)

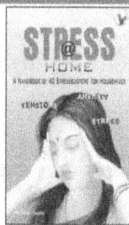

00401 P • ₹ 135 • 184 pp

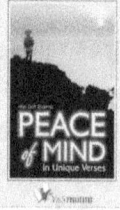

4021D • ₹ 96 • 174 pp

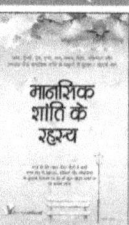

10402 P • ₹ 80 • 112 pp

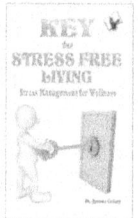

00403 P • ₹ 150 • 136 pp

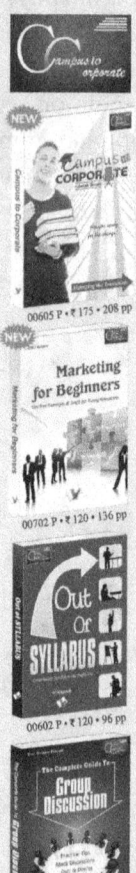

00605 P • ₹ 175 • 208 pp

00702 P • ₹ 120 • 136 pp

00602 P • ₹ 120 • 96 pp

00601 P • ₹ 135 • 190 pp

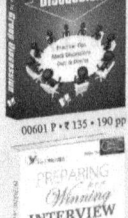

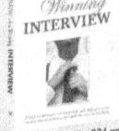

00603 P • ₹ 150 • 224 pp

All books available at www.vspublishers.com

PERSONALITY DEVELOPMENT
(व्यक्तित्व विकास)

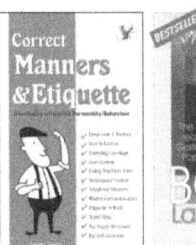

00306 P • ₹ 96 • 156 pp

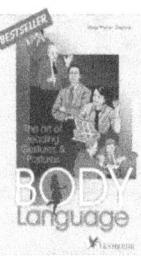

00302 P • ₹ 108 • 120 pp

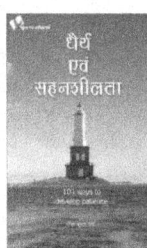

10208 P • ₹ 96 • 152 pp

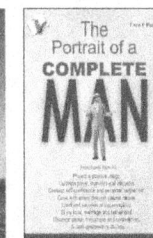

8995 D • ₹ 110 • 176 pp

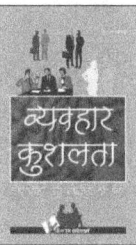

8911 D • ₹ 60 • 128 pp

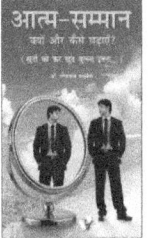

10302 P • ₹ 96 • 112 pp

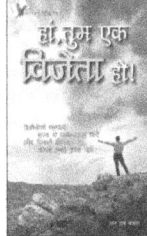

10214 P • ₹ 96 • 160 pp

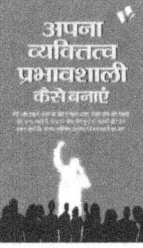

10304 P • ₹ 88 • 142 pp

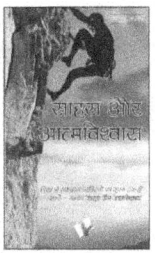

10307 P • ₹ 80 • 128 pp

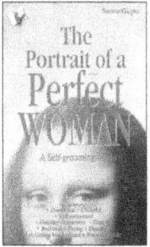

9062 B • ₹ 96 • 136 pp

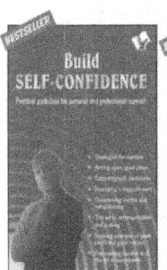

00301 P • ₹ 96 • 120 pp

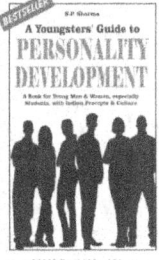

00303 P • ₹ 110 • 120 pp

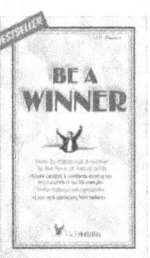

00606 P • ₹ 110 • 136 pp

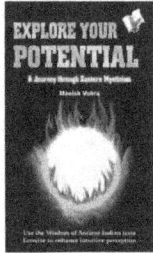

02801 P • ₹ 150 • 128 pp

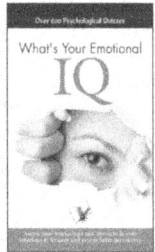

00305 P • ₹ 120 • 176 pp

Quick-bite to shake off sloth and lethargy and get cracking on your tasks and goals in life right away for self confidence, success and satisfaction. Liberally sprinkled with stories, anecdotes and events of ordinary people who achieved greatness.

The book provides high-value succinct guidelines on all matters of interest to students and job seeking professionals such as, personality development, etiquette and personal presentation for success in career and life.

Excel in your career! With inputs from hundreds of real-life examples, learn to turn challenges into opportunities, each day, and come out a winner in your social, personal and professional life.

The book helps the reader to get access to wisdom of several scriptures in one piece. Several sutras which are normally only passed on in the oral tradition are documented in the book.

Precise, accurate and to-the-point compilation of 600 psychological quizzes reveal your emotional IQ, an authoritative result which you can use to modify your attitude towards things that need betterment.

Contact us at sales@vspublishers.com

www.ingramcontent.com/pod-product-compliance
Lightning Source LLC
Chambersburg PA
CBHW052313220526
45472CB00001B/99